School Communication That Works

A Patron-Focused Approach to Delivering Your Message

Kenneth S. DeSieghardt

Published in partnership with NSPRA
ROWMAN & LITTLEFIELD EDUCATION
A division of
ROWMAN & LITTLEFIELD PUBLISHERS, INC.
Lanham • New York • Toronto • Plymouth, UK

Published in partnership with NSPRA

Published by Rowman & Littlefield Education
A division of Rowman & Littlefield Publishers, Inc.
A wholly owned subsidary of The Rowman & Littlefield Publishing Group, Inc.
4501 Forbes Boulevard, Suite 200, Lanham, Maryland 20706
www.rowman.com

10 Thornbury Road, Plymouth PL6 7PP, United Kingdom

British Library Cataloguing in Publication Information Available

Library of Congress Cataloging-in-Publication Data

Library of Congress Cataloging-in-Publication Data Available

ISBN 978-1-4758-0582-6 (cloth : alk. paper)—ISBN 978-1-4758-0583-3 (pbk. : alk. paper)—ISBN
978-1-4758-0584-0 (electronic)

∞™ The paper used in this publication meets the minimum requirements of American
National Standard for Information Sciences Permanence of Paper for Printed Library
Materials, ANSI/NISO Z39.48-1992.

Printed in the United States of America

Dedicated to educators everywhere, whose life work benefits us all.

Contents

Preface

Let's face it. No matter how long you've been a public education profession-al, you have had your moments of "wonder" when it comes to dealing with your patrons.

Perhaps it was an irate phone call, a chance meeting at the local grocery store, a comment said at a seemingly innocuous gathering of the parent group at one of your schools, and so on.

That comment could be the next verse of an all-too-familiar song, or it could be something that truly seems to come out of left field. After you deal with it as best as you can at that moment, you can't help but find yourself wondering, perhaps out loud, "Where did *that* come from?"

Then—more than likely—you wonder if you might have, could have, should have, said or done something differently, and whether the views just expressed by that patron are his or hers alone, or are indicative of the general views of your district community.

If you have those feelings, congratulations: you are a perfectly normal, well-adjusted public education leader who understands that schools are in the "business" of educating students and that you succeed in that business by building strong relationships with your "clients"—also known as your pa-trons.

The challenge is that while you undoubtedly feel as though you and your team have a firm grasp on the former, the latter can leave you scratching (or banging) your head at times. Just when you think you have begun to under-stand what makes your patron population tick, the phone rings, the e-mail click sounds, a patron starts a conversation with, "You may be the person to answer this question, because nobody else can. . . ." And the whole cycle of wonder (and worry) starts all over again.

Since 1992, I've crawled inside the heads, so to speak, of patrons in districts of all shapes, sizes, and socioeconomic conditions. I've asked them how they think their school district's people are performing, whether or not the school facilities are up to their expectations, if the programs are of suitable quality, and whether or not they feel that, as taxpayers, they are being both well served and understood, in addition to a myriad of other topics.

Most of the time, these questions have been part of research conducted to inform a school district's decision making about a potential ballot proposal. At other times, they have been part of a benchmark assessment that precedes a plan to strengthen district/patron relationships, or a follow-up study designed to check progress.

Over the course of this work, I've discovered that most patrons are passionately interested in a handful of topics related to their local school district and its performance, are moderately focused on another set, and don't think much at all about yet another group of topics.

While there are, of course, variations from district to district in the intensity of interest in certain topics, those differences are much more shades of gray than they are black and white.

Diving in deeper, I've discovered two other constants that can offer critical insights for district leaders trying to understand how their patrons think and trying to use that knowledge to more effectively communicate with their communities.

First, districts that struggle to develop and nurture strong relationships with their patrons tend to speak more in school jargon than they do in patron language.

By assuming that patrons are as interested as they are in the precise nuances of school business, a district all but assures itself that a significant majority of its community will press its mental mute button whenever someone from the district starts talking.

Face it: Our research says that 80 to 90 percent of your patrons are just not as interested in the details as you are, and nothing you can say or do will change that.

Second, patrons will never be completely comfortable and familiar with issues that, while important to how a school district functions, are still separated from the classroom. These include, but are not limited to, such things as how the board of education operates, the job the superintendent is doing, and whether or not the district keeps its promises.

Rightly or wrongly, patrons feel confident judging what takes place in the classroom. Even if they have no recent, direct experience (either through themselves or through the experiences of their own children), the performance of individual schools is enough of a topic of conversation among friends that most patrons seem to feel comfortable opining on the subject—even if they don't really have a leg to stand on.

We see it time and again in our research: teachers, quality of education, getting students ready for the next phase in their lives—anything within shouting distance of the classroom is fair game for patrons of all types to evaluate.

However, the other aspects of district life are a little harder to judge, say our research participants via their responses. For the majority, that means that their answer on a particular topic usually falls within one of the following groups:

- It's probably OK.
- It could probably get a little better.
- I don't know.

You may *think* that patrons should be interested in what the principals in your district are doing, the most recent board of education decision regarding an upcoming ballot issue, your new fourth-grade math curriculum, and so on, because these topics are essential to life in your district.

And, you'd be right: They *are* important. To you. But, they can be downright sleep-inducing to typical patrons.

Given those realities, what is a district to do?

Concentrate on communicating primarily about topics that are important to patrons, even though there's so much else you *could* say.

Remember that you are competing for your patrons' attention with (according to some experts) *three thousand other messages a day*. On that playing field, is it any wonder that patrons' eyes begin to glaze over when a district describing its upcoming ballot proposal thinks it's important to put a technically fine point on it by saying that it is a "debt extension," rather than simply stating that it "will mean no new taxes"?

"No new taxes" they get. "Debt extension" requires a detailed explanation that few patrons will take the time to review and understand.

This isn't to suggest that you hide anything. By all means, have the details on everything you do ready and available for those who *are* interested. But, don't force-feed that level of information to the masses. Again, 80 to 90 percent won't care about most of it, and you'll lose their interest (and, potentially, their advocacy) in the process.

Understanding what patrons do care about and what it means to you is the subject of this book. As you read this, you will likely have a few moments of clarity, some affirmation of what you already know, and some ideas that may challenge your thinking.

You may also find some information in here that you really doubt is accurate in terms of your patron population. That's understandable.

Some of the factors will shift around modestly from district to district, or even from time to time within your district. But, the basic principles of what's really important, and what's really of little to no interest to typical patrons in districts of all varieties, have proven consistent in research I've conducted since 1992.

The intent here is not to prove a thesis statement, but rather to help you focus your strategic and communications decision making on what matters most to patrons. Doing so will make you more effective and efficient, and will help your efforts to build and nurture the kind of district-patron relationships you seek.

It should also help lessen the frequency of those moments of "wonder."

Introduction

If you dog-ear this book, scribble notes in the margin, and turn down the pages (both the ones you like and the ones you may disagree with), then it will be serving its purpose.

You see, I didn't set out to produce a tome that would generate a lot of scholarly beard-stroking. Instead, I wanted to take what we had learned through our research at Patron Insight, and put it into a workbook-style format for public school leaders who want to find a way to translate the great work being done every day in their districts into messages that draw patrons in, keep their attention, and serve as yet another building block of a powerful district brand.

Great school district brands—meaning the feelings, emotions, and ideas that come to mind when a patron thinks about the district—are what get everyone (generally speaking) pulling in the same direction. It's what draws people to school board meetings, for all the right reasons. It's what gets ballot issues passed, and so on.

That objective should be your one-sentence communications plan: Build the school district's brand with stakeholders who are important to our success.

If that's your umbrella statement, you can use this book (and its reporting of the experiences of your fellow school districts) to help you organize your thinking on how to do just that.

In the pages that follow, you will see some thinking on the differences between passionate and what we call "typical" patrons, and how to direct your communications at the masses (because the positive and negative zealots will always be with you—for better or worse).

We then present the findings from our research in one simple illustration, which we call the "Patron Information Pyramid™." It's an approach that can help as you decide how to allocate resources, but—as is mentioned throughout this book—it is intended to serve as a guide, not a hard and fast rulebook for communications success. Use it as you sort through your thinking to create and execute your district's unique communications plan.

Following the Pyramid presentation are individual chapters focusing on the topics you *could* talk about, in descending order from most to least important, with some ideas (again, drawn from what patrons have told us in our research) about what you should be talking about on each subject. There are also some thoughts on how to handle hot topics, and how to approach crisis communications from a patron-focused perspective.

Like the dinner-hour speaker who goes into an event hoping that his or her guests leave with a tip or two that they can use right away, my goal is to help you see how successful district-patron relationships start when you let *patrons* dictate your communications strategy and tactics.

Chapter One

The 80/20 Rule

There's a familiar maxim in business that goes something like this: "20 percent of your customers account for 80 percent of your business."

It's a tried-and-true reminder that a business's best opportunities for meaningful growth come from those who are already active, engaged customers, because the cost of encouraging more purchases from already-satisfied customers is a fraction of what it takes to build and nurture new relationships.

Of course, this doesn't mean that a business should ignore the great unwashed who may not have discovered yet how much they need the widget that the company is peddling. It's simply the fact that the cost of adding these new customers is typically far greater than the cost of convincing those already in the know to buy more from you.

The intent of this guideline is to focus a business's time, energy, and resources where the greatest opportunity for a meaningful net return exists.

Our research has discovered that school districts have their own 80/20 rule of sorts.

Specifically, school districts typically obsess over the thoughts, ideas, concerns, and opinions of the 20 percent of patrons (a majority of whom are parents) who make it a point to speak up regularly, while assuming that all is—for the most part—fine with the 80 percent of citizens who rarely, if ever, say a word.

In a general sense, and using round numbers, half of that 20 percent are the people I call "The Happys" (please excuse the unique spelling).

"The Happys" are those smiling folks who are the first to sign up to volunteer, who are always at the PTO or PTA meetings, who are always popping in to school to enjoy a noon meal with their child or to thank a teacher for special attention, who are always writing letters to the editor championing the district, and so on.

They're your raving fans. They're well-known and appreciated at the building level, and the true stars of this group are also known at the district level, because they've made it clear that they "will do anything for the schools." The Happys are the people that you start each day hoping you'll see or hear from, because they're great morale boosters around the central office or in your school buildings.

The other half of that 20 percent are—as you probably guessed—"The Unhappys" (again, my apologies for the spelling liberties).

"The Unhappys" are also first. They're first to stand up with the dicey question at the open house. First to call you when something doesn't seem quite right to them. First to speak negatively about your bond issue. First to say "no" when asked to join a committee. First to speak during the public comment time at the board of education meeting (often on the same topic they talked about last month). You get the idea.

The Unhappys are the ones most likely to cause you to lose sleep, because nothing you do seems to satisfy them. It's never the answer they are looking for (or, most of the time, the one they are *hoping* for), and the more you leave them unsatisfied, the more they seem to find fault.

So, it's only human nature that you relish the encounters with The Happys and gird yourself for interactions with The Unhappys.

And who gets lost in that equation? The 80 percent of your patrons that you never hear from.

Research backs up what would seem to be common sense when it comes to these groups and their attitudes toward your district.

Specifically, unless you do something that deliberately alienates The Happys, they'll remain your fans for life. Think about it: how much turnover is there at your local building PTOs or PTAs (aside from the times when those leaders move up to the next building level with their sons and daughters)?

By the same token, there is no way to please a true member of The Unhappys.

In a twist on the old breakup line, in this case, "It's not you, it's *them*." They are who they are because they enjoy a scrap, or maybe because they didn't get their way once in school, and this is their chance to get back at someone in authority. They can't seem to understand the word *no*, whatever the case may be. Every story is different, but the result is the same: they like being a thorn in the school district's side.

Knowing this, why is it that so many school districts focus their emotional energy and resources on The Happys and The Unhappys (the 20 percent from the 80/20 rule)—when it's the opinions of those you never hear from that you need to understand, and it's their support that you need to cultivate?

More than likely, it's because understanding this silent (but vast) majority seems like an impossible task. They never show up for public meetings, never leave you a voicemail or send you an e-mail, never set foot in any one of your buildings (expect, perhaps, at parent-teacher conference time), never come to a sporting event, and never volunteer for anything.

All they seem to do is vote. And that's where they make their voices heard.

Are they trying to be mysterious? For the most part, no.

The truth is that most of this 80 percent majority is so busy with other things in their lives that *they cherry-pick a handful of items as ways to judge whether schools, and the district leaders who run them, are doing a good job.*

(This is much, much different than The Happys and The Unhappys, who regularly review your budget, your staffing plans, the books on your library shelves, the policies of your coaches regarding playing time, etc. They live to praise or criticize, and they want to be well armed when they do either.)

In other words, if the things that matter most to this silent majority appear to be functioning effectively, then they'll generally think that everything else is running smoothly.

They may not be active advocates, but they are more likely to give you the benefit of the doubt on most topics—if they believe that the district's performance is acceptable-to-exemplary in the areas they care about.

For school district leaders who are excited about the work they do and who want to share each and every detail with their patrons, this can be rather discouraging news. But study after study that we've conducted—in districts from very large and urban, to tiny and rural—backs up this sobering assertion: your patrons don't care as much as you do.

Knowing this, you have two choices.

Choice A is to try to *make* them care, by overwhelming them with data and with reasons why they should care. This is the "If they only knew, they would care" approach, and it's all wrong.

Why? Because it violates the basic principle of communication:

The sender of the information must communicate something that interests the listener. No interest equals no listening.

Like it or not, the 80 percent who reside in the middle aren't interested in much detail. They already tune you out now on most areas—except the ones they care about—and you can't change that by shoveling more data in their direction. So stop trying to "convert" them.

It's the same reason that BMW doesn't try to win over Kia drivers, and vice versa. While you may occasionally see a Kia driver with a big, fat company bonus check on the showroom floor at the local BMW shop, or a recently unemployed BMW driver who finds it necessary to downsize his or her ride, both companies know that if they tried to talk to someone who's not inclined to listen, they would be wasting their time and money. They save the details for the 20 percent, and pick up some of the remaining 80 percent by chance.

Choice B, on the other hand, involves focusing the majority of your communications and your efforts to nurture district-patron relationships on the topics that *are* of interest to this large audience, and bringing them "into the tent" that way. This doesn't mean that you ignore the other great news that you have to share; you just don't spotlight it quite as frequently, or as aggressively, as you may want to.

The good news in Choice B is twofold.

First, members of the 80 percent group will start thinking, "Hey, the district knows the things that interest me," and will begin to pay closer attention to what you have to say on all fronts.

Second, your Happys and Unhappys will still be right there, soaking it all in. (No, there is no magic communications formula that makes the Unhappys go away or that changes their minds.)

Sound easy? It isn't.

You know how good your district is, and you are very familiar with all the great news you could share to prove that point. Leaving some of that information on the shelf when you speak to your patron population requires discipline.

Worse yet, you will get tired of hearing yourself talk about the same subjects (same song, different verse, each time) over and over again. You'll think to yourself, "Can't I say something else?"

The short answer is *yes*. Again, this isn't a case of shutting off the spigot of information. It's a matter of simply finding the right balance of hot and cold water that will make the largest number of your patrons sit up and take notice.

It's sort of the school-district version of what advertising icon David Ogilvy said when asked about his definition of *marketing*.

Ogilvy said, "Marketing is finding out what people want and giving them more of it, and finding out what they don't want and giving them less of it."

Your communications should follow the principles of this simple, yet powerful, definition. And on the pages that follow, we'll discuss what our research suggests that patrons in districts large, small, and in between have said they want "more of."

Chapter Two

Patron-Speak versus District-Speak

A Primer

Within my first week at the public relations agency where I would soon become immersed in public education, I found myself leading a meeting with a long-time health care client who had arrived at our shop to hear our recommendations for their annual fall advertising campaign.

I saw that meeting as an important moment in my time with the agency, and I wanted to make a powerful impression on the client, and on the president of my firm. For the client: *You can have confidence in me and my recommendations.* For the president: *You've made a good choice by adding me to the staff.*

So, I deftly (or so I thought) facilitated a meeting, using phrases such as, "I've been thinking about your fall campaign" (which I had) and "From my experience, I think you should really focus on hand-picking certain specialties that would offer your entire hospital a real 'halo' benefit. I think that if you focus on cardiology, for example, residents will have a better impression about all that you have to offer."

The client committed to considering the campaign idea that I had presented, and I left the meeting beaming about my performance, only to be met in the hallway by our firm's president. He wanted to have . . . a chat.

That "chat" went something like this: "You made no effort to connect with what matters to that client. You jumped right into the solution without showing him that you understood his needs and his expectations. You left the efforts of the team totally out of the conversation. This wasn't a sales presentation, Ken. It was a chance to continue to build a relationship with this client, by showing how much we understand his needs."

Gulp.

He was right, of course. In my attempt to show confidence, I had turned what should have been a client-focused conversation into a bit of a show-piece for what I was bringing to the party. In doing so, I was talking, instead of communicating.

(For the record: I survived that day, and ended up thriving there for eight years, growing more passionate about public education month by month, thanks to the great school district clients we were fortunate to be able to serve.)

Talking is about all you. And, all too often, well-intentioned school districts do *a lot* of talking.

"We follow a Professional Learning Community model." "We are chang-ing the 'bell schedule' and starting school one hour late each Thursday so that our teachers have dedicated 'collaboration time.'" "We are working on a five-year strategic plan." And so on, and so on.

Oftentimes, this habit of "talking" comes from the best intentions: public education professionals usually adore their work and are genuinely excited about the impact they are making on the lives of children, families, and communities.

That's certainly the type of person I want teaching my children and lead-ing my school district.

However, that enthusiasm often causes these same professionals to as-sume that stakeholders will be equally fascinated by all the machinations associated with school district life. That can lead to feature-focused, jargon-filled communications output that does a great job of documenting district activities and plans, but typically does little to help build and nurture a meaningful connection.

Think of it as "reporting," rather than "engaging."

As is mentioned throughout this book, our research in districts large, small, and in between shows a consistent pattern of thought from patrons:

Talk to me about what interests me, not about what interests you.

Such a dictate is easy to follow, of course, when the news you want to share has an obvious connection to patron interests. Student awards, high performance on test scores, and the grand opening of new facilities are among the slam-dunks.

But, what about news that can't be captured with a simple "Huzzah!"-type headline, or with a grip-and-grin photo (I know, "Ugh!") of a happy student and his or her smiling parents? How do you transform dry data, plans, and other such information into patron-focused content?

First, take a step back and double-check your thinking. Your distr. website is a great repository for plans, budget details, technology updates, and such. Zealots will easily find that information there, meaning that you will have addressed the data needs of your most ardent followers.

But before you go actively pushing upper-tier stories on five-year plans, budget breakdowns, and the like to a mass audience, consider the risks and rewards of your efforts, and the makeup of your stakeholder groups. Have they been clamoring for such detail, or are you likely to only confuse those who have a typical level of interest—and unintentionally distance yourself from them in the process?

Also, is now the right time? Or, will the story be better, more detailed, or more finalized at some point in the future? Is a full-blown treatment the best approach, or would a tweet with a link to the details on your website suffice, for example?

In other words—is this important to your stakeholders, or is it just important to you?

You can't push the toothpaste back into the tube, and a clumsy or ill-timed release of complicated material will do more long-term harm than good among those who pay a typical level of attention to what the school district says. So take a moment or two and run through the plan one more time, just to make certain it's the right thing to do.

If you do decide to proceed, here's more advice from our research participants about how to connect with them:

Lead with benefits, and follow with features.

"Smart Boards Now Part of Every Classroom in Smith Elementary School" is a headline you can see yourself writing, can't you? After all, you know what a Smart Board is, how it works, and the opportunities it presents for creative presentations by teachers and students.

But, that's because Smart Boards are a part of your world, perhaps every day. Your teachers have been itching to have the technology added. It's been a regular topic of conversation. So, of course, everyone will know what you mean. Right?

Probably not. When you take a step back and think about your patron population, the chances are good that less than half of your households have a current district student living in them. As such, this news is not something they can relate to, because they don't have children coming home talking about "using the Smart Board in class."

r focus with a headline like this, instead: "Students Have
es to Showcase Their Creativity, Thanks to New Technolo-
:ntary School."

bvious: The "why" comes before the "what." Enhancing
student creativity is the story, and the Smart Boards are the reason. It's a
better way to get the attention of both your current parents and of patrons
who have no connection to the district right now—other than the fact that
they pay taxes.

And, it doesn't just work with technology stories:

"Getting Ready for the Needs of Today's and Tomorrow's Students Is
Focus of Five-Year Planning Process," instead of "District Launches Five-
Year Facility Planning Initiative."

"Keeping Reasonable Class Sizes Drives Budget Planning Team's
Work," instead of "Budget Planning Process Sets Maintaining Class Sizes as
a High Priority."

"Spanish Students to Have a Real-Life Opportunity to Test Their Skills,"
instead of "Trip Details for High School Spanish Students Being Finalized."

The actual news ("getting ready," "keeping class sizes reasonable," "have
a real-life opportunity") comes first, then the tangible details. This goes for
headlines, tweets, Facebook posts, website mentions—everything. If the typical patron wouldn't at least pause to glance at your headline, you need to
change it.

Tell them "what this means."

When we're conducting research designed to help a school district and/or
its planning committees whittle down a wish list to a more manageable
number of project ideas, we typically ask our survey participants what, if
anything, they may have already heard about the planning work that has been
taking place. The responses provide a window into the effectiveness of the
district's communications to date about this process.

Many times, the leading response (after "I haven't heard anything," or
words to that effect) is something along the lines of "They are working on a
plan" or "They have had meetings to talk about the future of the district."
Responses like this suggest that awareness of this planning effort is probably
the result of conversations with a chatty neighbor or a scan of "news" from
Facebook friends, rather than evidence that a district has been successful in
making this news meaningful to the masses.

In other cases, however, a notable number of research participants can not
only name for us the specific ideas that are being discussed, but they often
phrase their awareness using a hint of benefit language, such as, "They are
talking about building a new middle school to deal with the crowding issue."

The stakeholders in the latter example have a deeper understanding of the work underway, because the district has made a conscious effort to fill in all the blanks by explaining what the planning effort means to patrons, their families, their schools, the community, and so on.

The phrase "what this means" is a very disarming way to get the benefit points across, because it's so conversational. But even more important is how it can be a quality-control mechanism as a school district prepares to communicate something substantive. If you haven't explained "what this means" to your target audience, then there is still work to do, say our research participants.

Focus quotes on "you" statements, not "we" proclamations.

Like the example above from the early days of my career, it's the rare person who enjoys a conversation with someone who talks incessantly about himself or herself, and never inquires about the listener's well-being. Tolerate? Maybe. But, not enjoy.

So, keep that mindset in place as you consider quotes you will include from district leaders, principals, or anyone else who has something to contribute to the news being shared.

For example, saying, "Putting struggling students in a position to succeed is the purpose of this program," sends an outward benefit message, while "This program was designed by the district to help struggling students succeed" makes the district's action the focus.

The issue here is how quotes can draw people to your news (and, in turn, your district) or repel them.

Making the quote about the district creates distance, and is as boring and unlikable as the cocktail party guest with a billfold full of photos of his children to share. Making it about students, teachers, schools, or the community puts the district (and, in turn, the person attached to the quote) in the role of *enabler*. And, in this case, that's a good thing.

Don't expect stakeholders to remember. *Anything.*

The final piece of advice gleaned from our research with patrons is a simple one: they won't remember what you said, so don't count on it.

This is a painful lesson that can sour the stomachs of school district communications professionals and central office leadership, who work tirelessly to shape messages, perfect timing, and aggressively disseminate data, only to hear a patron say, "I never heard anything about X or Y or Z."

As such, when it comes to complex, ongoing, or multi-part stories, patrons have said they would appreciate a reminder about any news that came before that is connected to the story of the day.

In other words, if you are promoting a Town Hall meeting to talk about plans for an upcoming ballot issue—and it's the third of three such meetings—sprinkling in information that was shared, and questions that were asked, in the previous two meetings will bring a first-time reader up to speed.

Think of this a bit like television shows that begin with a quick recap of any pertinent scenes from the last episode or two that part-time viewers might have missed. They're trying to make it easier for someone who has been away for a while (or someone who is watching for the first time) to follow the story, and they don't expect viewers to commit all the details from the past shows to memory.

If television viewers need a refresher before watching a sitcom, what makes school districts think that patrons can recite the nuances of the five-year plan they've told them about?

KEY POINTS:

- Talking meets the needs of the message sender, but communicating is focused on making a connection with the recipient and what matters to him or her. Make sure that your interaction with patrons and other key stakeholder groups is true communication.
- Every aspect of school district life is not worthy of active communications. Overwhelming stakeholders with detailed information about plans, meeting minutes, and similar material (that could, instead, be placed on your website for the interested minority) will make it more difficult to get their attention.
- Patron-focused language is benefit-driven, and positions the school district (or a school, a principal, a teacher, and so on) as the enabler of that benefit. The same guideline goes for district representatives who are quoted in your outbound news.
- Make certain that your communications can answer the "What this means" test for key stakeholders. If not, there's still work to do.
- Repeat, refresh, and remind whenever you have a complicated story that you need to tell over an extended time period. Assuming that your patrons remember nothing about what you've said in the past is the safest way to proceed.

This is how patrons think: *Show me—right away—why I should pay attention to what you are sharing. Tell me how your news will benefit my child, our family, his or her school, and our community—in that order.*

Spend less time talking about yourself, your accomplishments, and your plans, and more time talking about what matters to me. (And if you don't know what matters to me, ask.)

Chapter Three

The Patron Information Pyramid

Step into any first-year high school journalism classroom, and you'll hear about the "inverted pyramid."

Simply stated, the concept says that when you are writing a story for the media—whether it be print, broadcast, online, or whatever—you should put all the most important facts at the beginning, and place the details deeper into the story. The idea is that if you get a reader, listener or viewer to only *glance* at your story, you need to give him or her the salient points right away, and leave the details for those who are interested enough to keep reading, watching, or listening.

Coined long before our collective attention spans devolved to eight-second sound bites, headlines on a crawl across the television screen, or snippets on the web, the inverted pyramid is as much a sales strategy for capturing the attention of the broadest target audience as it is a journalistic principle.

Journalists then and now know that they are competing for your attention, so they have to give you a reason to care about what they have to say.

That *reason* goes first in the story ("Stock market takes a nosedive!"), followed by exactly how much of a dive it was, which types of stocks took the biggest hit, and so on.

In the world of school districts and the information they have to share, the principle of the inverted pyramid applies as well—but with a twist. *What goes at the top of this inverted pyramid should be dictated by what patrons think is important—whether or not the district sees it the same way.*

That's a statement that's likely to upend more than a few school district communication plans out there. Patrons *should* be extremely interested in every nook and cranny of school district life, right? After all, it is their tax dollars we're spending, so shouldn't we go out of our way to prove that we're worth what they're investing?

In theory, yes. After all, schools are the foundation of great communities, so understanding the details about what is going on in your local school district—so that you, as a taxpayer, can get involved—should be important. But sadly, it isn't.

Once, again, you're left with the choice of force-feeding information that *you* think is important, or following what we call the "Patron Information Pyramid." Our research will tell you that the latter is the way to go for your district's health, for your budget, and for your sanity.

The Patron Information Pyramid looks like this:

The Patron Information Pyramid™

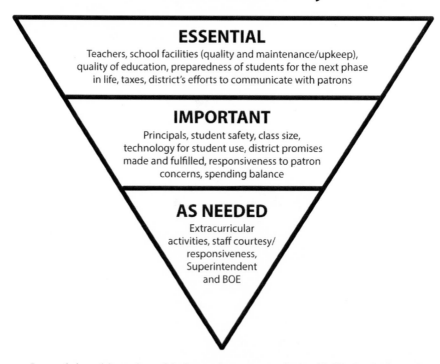

ESSENTIAL
Teachers, school facilities (quality and maintenance/upkeep), quality of education, preparedness of students for the next phase in life, taxes, district's efforts to communicate with patrons

IMPORTANT
Principals, student safety, class size, technology for student use, district promises made and fulfilled, responsiveness to patron concerns, spending balance

AS NEEDED
Extracurricular activities, staff courtesy/ responsiveness, Superintendent and BOE

In studying this order of information, your mind will likely drift to that "frequent flyer" patron who always signs up to speak at your board of education meetings. Or the one who is constantly haranguing your best principal over the math curriculum the district is using. Or the one who constantly sends you statistics about how students who use Macintosh computers in school fare better on college entrance exams than do those who "are *forced* to use a PC," and so on.

These are the 20 percent of your patrons mentioned earlier in this book. They're familiar to you, because they are always in your face. But, their level of specific interest is atypical in terms of your total patron population.

Helping you put that call, e-mail, or encounter into perspective is what the Patron Information Pyramid is all about.

But, in saying that, it is important to remember that the Pyramid is not a recipe, but rather a guideline. There will always be cases in which, for example, a topic will move around the Patron Information Pyramid—particularly between the middle and bottom levels. It could be a short-term outlier, or something that is unique to your district.

That's OK. The Pyramid comes from research findings, and it's meant to guide you on the most important *outgoing* communications—not to provide you with an escape clause for dealing with challenges initiated by patrons.

In essence, the average patron is most interested in the basics of school district life: teachers, buildings, good value for the tax dollars they are spending, and if the district is delivering a good education that prepares students to be a success — whether those students become lawyers, plumbers, or anything else.

Those are the issues that, in their minds, define a quality school district.

Of more modest importance—but still important, at varying levels—are student safety (remember, this is an aggregate of findings from urban, suburban, and rural districts conducted before, during, and after safety stories that made national headlines; a *general* expectation of safety is assumed in most districts), principals, class sizes (again, unless there's a problem), technology that students have available to use, whether or not you keep your promises, and whether you spend your money equitably and appropriately across all the places it could be spent.

The least important factors are the ones that are, in the minds of typical patrons, a couple of steps removed from the primary educational function of schools. Extracurricular activities; courtesy of the staff; and the performance of the superintendent, board of education, and the central office staff just don't register for most patrons—unless there's a problem.

This is often the hardest concept for superintendents and members of the board to wrap their collective heads around.

Why? Because they hear from patrons all the time—either directly via phone, fax, e-mail, or in person; or anonymously, such as via a comment on the blog of the local newspaper, for example.

But, like understanding the difference between "total visits" to a website and "unique visitors," it's important to put the volume of comments from patrons in the proper context.

Our patron research has confirmed that critics are much more likely to speak up about the district and its leadership on a broad swath of issues, than they are to focus on one area where they may have a complaint. If you forget that context, it's easy to get swept up in the notion that *everyone* is fixated on what the district's leadership is up to.

But that same research shows, on average, that 25 percent to as much as 45 percent of patrons have no opinion about the work of the board of education or the superintendent, for example. Again, if there's no reason (such as a controversy) for the average patron to be interested, he or she won't be, while the rest typically evaluate the performance as being at or above average—or admit that they don't know enough to offer an opinion.

The message: What happens in the classroom (or what patrons *think* happens in the classroom) matters most, along with whether or not a school district is careful with the patrons' money, and keeps those same patrons relatively informed. Everything else is supplemental data in the typical patron's mind.

As such, these are the topics that, if they are the focus of your communications initiatives, can help you build and nurture stronger relationships with patrons of all types.

In the chapters that follow, we'll break down the three tiers in the Patron Information Pyramid, and discuss what patrons have told us they want to hear about for each component found therein.

Chapter Four

The Top Tier of the Pyramid

Essential Information

In our research endeavors, we encourage (alright, it's more like *insist*) our school district clients to begin each research study by allowing their patrons the opportunity to give the district a rating on a variety of different people, program, and facility areas, and on several key components of the district-patron relationship.

When we first began our work with schools, the initial part of a survey planning meeting with a school district would involve a review of a rather scant list of items that we thought should be included in this exercise—along with an invitation to those in attendance to add to that list, if there was something missing they wanted patrons to evaluate.

As ideas were shared over the years, the list grew. Today, it's grown so long—thanks to the good ideas of our clients—that it's now divided into "important" and "other" items, and it remains a staple of our process.

As we completed each research project, we reported the items that generated high scores, those that generated modest (but still positive) ratings, and those for which the scores seemed to suggest a concern.

We also noted the people, program, facility, and district-patron relationship areas in which at least 81 percent of participants felt confident enough in their knowledge (whether it was directly obtained, or it was second-hand) to offer a rating, rather than saying "I don't know."

The idea behind these "Patron Hot Buttons," as we call them, is simple. If more than four out of five patrons—no matter what their connection to the school district might be (current parent, parent of a former student, future parent, grandparent, or simply a taxpayer)—have an opinion on a particular

15

topic area, than that topic has separated itself as being much, much more important than average to that patron community.

Those things that *patrons* deem most important are the areas where school districts should be placing their communications attention, while lesser areas should get an appropriately diminished amount of communications time and energy.

That's when true communication happens: *When the information transmitted matters to the recipients* **(no matter how the "transmitter" may feel about its relative importance in the grand scheme of things).**

Another key component: consistency.

The problem for most school districts is that they reach a point where they think they've completed the communications task, and they take their foot off the gas and start talking in overwhelming frequency and detail about other things.

Advertising people will tell you that a person has to be exposed to the same message at least six times before he or she even remembers who is delivering the message, let alone what the message is saying. When I was in the advertising business, we used to describe it this way to clients: "When you are absolutely sick and tired of saying the same thing over and over again, your target audience is finally starting to see it and hear it for the first time."

This means that communicating information related to the Patron Hot Buttons has no finish line. It's a daily task.

So, what are the areas that patrons—time and again, no matter what their connection to the school district may be at the time we contact them—consider the most important in judging a quality school district from an also-ran? There are six that have routinely bubbled to the top since 1992, and are, therefore, considered Essential Information by patrons.

Chapter Five

Essential Information

Value for the Tax Dollars Spent

At a planning meeting, the outcome of which would guide the creation of a pre-election research study, I had a board of education member ask me a somewhat rhetorical question: "Have you ever, in all your years of working with school districts, run into a patron who thought they didn't pay enough in taxes?"

The answer, of course, was "no." But, as I explained to the board member, it's not a simple "no," as in "No, I'm looking to cut my tax bill any way that I can, no matter what it may mean."

Rather, the issue, it seems, is less a concern about the concept of *paying* taxes to support the school district, and more about having to foot the bill for a district that doesn't seem to be effective in delivering *on what I consider to be important.*

While The Unhappys that I mentioned earlier will scrutinize every penny of the taxes they pay to the school district (and to everyone else, for that matter), the typical patron isn't concerned until something causes him or her to question the value he or she is getting for what is being spent.

That's the key word: *value*.

Time and again, patrons in our research have said that it's not a case of how big the tax bill is, but whether or not they *believe* the school district is making generally smart financial choices. Interestingly, this belief isn't typically impacted by the actual size of the tax bill paid to the school district.

Whether the district is frugal, free-spending, or somewhere in the middle, our research tells us that patrons have the same litmus test: *What am I getting for my money?*

So, what do patrons define as "good tax value" investments?

Generally, *anything that involves maintenance or renovation of existing facilities is seen as a good value.* That's because patrons see the school district behaving as they would with upkeep needs on their own homes.

They keep their homes in good mechanical shape, and make certain that they are aesthetically acceptable, because it protects their investment. By the same token, they've already invested in the schools, so changes like these are seen as protecting that investment.

Expansion is just a step below, on the typical patron's value equation.

Expansion is clearly more expensive than just sprucing up what you have, so it's critical that the "we need to expand" story doesn't arrive cold, but is allowed to simmer over time. This means that a steady diet of information about enrollment trends, crowded classrooms, population shifts, and the like is an essential component of the strategy to make an expansion proposal more palatable.

A more difficult sale—no matter what the economy—is new facilities. But, even that's not an absolute.

Our research has found that patrons in certain districts may have no qualms whatsoever about building a new building practically every year to deal with growth and to keep up with the Joneses in the district next door, while others will look at a ninety-year-old school building that's barely had a coat of paint in the last fifty years and say, "It was good enough for me. It's good enough for the kids today."

Therein lies the rub: common sense doesn't always win out.

Case in point: We worked on research for a district with a middle school built in 1918 that was desperately in need of replacement—which should go without saying.

It was more than an eyesore; it was a hazard. Bathrooms barely functional. An HVAC system that was the equivalent of leaving the windows open in the winter. Rickety, makeshift ADA accommodations. You get the idea.

So they created a sensible plan that would result in a functional—but frugal—new school, and that would then turn over the existing building to the county, which would renovate it modestly to use as community meeting space.

No sale, said the research. Patrons said that education was "what happens *in* the classroom, not the classroom itself," and they pointed to the district's habit of winning awards for its academic excellence.

(There's the ultimate double-edged sword, isn't it? Win awards for your performance, and patrons could assume that nothing needs to be improved.

Fall short, and they might not be willing to invest more money in a "failing" school district!)

Lost on these patrons was the fact that those award-winning teachers wouldn't be staying forever in a facility that, to put it very kindly, was substandard, if the community didn't care enough to provide them and their students with competent working conditions.

On the other hand, other districts for which we've conducted research are populated by very competitive patrons who think new buildings are essential to a quality education. In some cases, they need to keep contractors busy just to keep up with enrollment. In others, it's more a matter of pride.

Where does your district stand? That depends on what your patrons expect and the role that they believe facilities play in a quality education. It's important to get a clear understanding of their mood on that subject through research, so that you can deliver the right value message.

Whichever definition best fits your patrons, the key to successful communication about new facilities is to target your messages to the 80 percent of your patrons who want the basic information ("We need this new school, *because it will relieve the overcrowding in the northeast part of the district*"), while also preparing all the details for those who want to dive deep into everything related to the district.

Remember, when it comes to information, you need to live in their world. Don't ask them to live in yours.

The toughest "value" sale? Any facility that patrons believe will impact only a percentage of students, or that benefits only district leadership.

So this means that facilities such as natatoriums (also known as swimming pools), performing arts centers (PACs), new central office buildings, new stadiums, and artificial turf installation at existing stadiums can be trouble spots. With rare exceptions (such as football stadiums at Texas high schools), these facilities are generally the lowest on the patron value meter—particularly if said patron has no children in school at the present time.

This isn't to say that projects such as these are always a lost cause, however. It's just that the value message a district might deliver on, for example, artificial turf (pays for itself over time; field is always available for teams, band, etc.,) will take more time to resonate with a typical patron than a project with benefits that are clearly more broad-based, such as added classrooms at an overcrowded school.

Beyond the brick-and-mortar projects, patrons have a separate value equation when it comes to ongoing operating expenses.

While there are some districts whose patrons would like their teachers to be at the top of the pay scale in their region (and others at the opposite end of the spectrum, who think that teachers have it easy, because "they only work nine months out of the year"), we've found in our research that preaching a goal of "competitive" salaries for teachers and staff rings true for most tax-payers.

The power of the word "competitive" in this situation comes from its generally accepted definition. Sports teams that don't win all their games—but tend to make a good showing each time on the field, court, rink, etc.—are considered competitive. Corporate salary structures are set up to be some-where in the middle, to just above the middle, of the pack. Talk to any human resources professional in the corporate world, and they'll tell you that they don't need to lead in terms of salaries; they just need to be "competitive" to attract top talent.

So it's only natural that this type of messaging is a good fit with the sensibilities of patrons.

Another message that squares with their thought process, according to our research, deals with the funds that will be used to pay for the increasing costs of basic school necessities, such as energy costs for buildings, fuel for buses, textbooks for the classroom, and the like.

While we've found that every community has a small subset of patrons who will say, "We all have to tighten our belts; the school district should have to also!" most have told us through our research that they can relate.

Again, the message that finds favor focuses on *keeping up with the rising costs of necessities*—not on getting ahead. It's the operating-expense equivalent of "protecting what you've already invested in."

Case in point: We worked with one district that asked patrons to support an increase in the operating levy that would bring it up to the middle of the pack on salaries and—more importantly—keep it from having to eliminate two hundred positions, which would have ballooned class sizes.

Even though the requested increase was fairly modest, the district was hit by the double whammy of a drying-up job market in town and growing awareness that it had some $35 million in reserves. The typical patron said, "You've got $35 million. Why are you asking me for more?"

The school district's sound business management practices came back to bite it, because patrons hadn't been steadily (and simply) schooled on why having a solid reserve account is a critical component of fiscal responsibility. Once the "they already have a ton of money" rumble gained traction in the community, the proposal was doomed.

Another district we worked with faced a different challenge when asking for an increase to its operating levy. Specifically, it had been *too quiet* about what it had already done to trim its budget, meaning that the request for more funds risked being a complete "Where did this come from?" situation for patrons.

Our research on behalf of that district revealed a generally satisfied patron population that was modestly supportive of the idea of a fairly hefty increase in the operating tax levy. But our questions that asked the district's patrons to judge the level of community awareness regarding the district's financial plight (which is a researcher's way of asking someone what he or she knows without putting him or her on the spot), showed a disconcerting lack of familiarity.

They didn't know that the district had been all that frugal, didn't know about the cuts that had been made (beyond the general awareness that "things are tough for schools"), and didn't have any idea about the train that was barreling down the tracks in the district's direction, if nothing was done to supplement the bottom line.

The campaign committee took this data to heart, and laid out a very simple message that detailed what had taken place to date, the impact of those changes, and the draconian cuts that were being discussed. Their focus wasn't on peddling fear—which, we've found, generally backfires—but on pushing pride. They said, in essence, "We're proud of our schools, and we'd like to maintain their quality. Here's a proposal to do just that."

In doing so, the committee brought the community quickly up to speed, made the case for the proposal very crisply and repetitively, and secured a win on Election Day—all because it matched its message to what patrons value.

KEY POINTS

- Patrons expect their school district to manage its money with the same general approach that they follow in their own lives.
- That's why they tend to overwhelmingly support renovation projects (fixing up what they've already paid for), followed by expansion, and then building new.
- They're generally more resistant to special facilities and projects (pools, PACs, artificial turf), but can soften if they see how these expenses will benefit more than the swim team, the drama department, or the football squad, for example. And, of course, there are regional differences that make such facilities critical to *passing* a ballot proposal, rather than putting the whole question at risk by including them.
- Patrons want to pay teachers and staff a fair wage, so that the good teachers don't leave, but they usually don't believe that unusually high salaries draw the best teachers and staff.
- They understand the reality that sometimes it takes more money to operate a school district than it used to. If they believe the district is generally frugal, they tend to support such a notion at the ballot box.

This is how patrons think: *Continually show me that you manage your money with an understanding that it is actually MY money, and I'll be much more likely to support you when you need additional funds.*

Do not wait until you need my support at the ballot box to start showcasing your fiscal prudence and the value you are delivering for the tax dollars I'm investing.

Chapter Six

Essential Information

Quality of School Facilities

If there's one issue that seems to polarize school district patrons like no other, it's the quality of their school facilities.

It's true that some suburban and so-called exurban districts have patrons who view the aesthetic qualities and amenities of their school buildings as a badge of honor that separates them from their equally competitive neighboring districts.

(As an example, we work with many districts whose newer high schools have permanent logo-wear stores inside the school building. The ever-more common existence of such facilities makes me wonder how I survived without daily access to the opportunity to purchase a Shawnee Mission West Vikings hoodie during my own high school career in the 1970s.)

But outside of the districts whose constituents expect what some might call "palaces" for their students, our research suggests that patrons tend to fall into one of three camps when it comes to what they consider suitable school facilities.

Occupants of Camp One bristle at the idea that children need shiny, new buildings to get a good education. Almost overwhelmingly, these are patrons whose children have long since left the (school) building, and many of these patrons occupied the very same school buildings during their own academic careers. They "remember when," and it kills them to hear the district saying that what was good enough when they or their children were taught is hopelessly out-of-date now. They simply choose not to acknowledge the problems.

Those in Camp Two hold the exact opposite view. They believe that up-to-date buildings and tools create a successful environment for students, teachers, and staff. They value computer labs with this year's hardware and software, science wings with equipment that would make some medical researchers salivate, PACs with lighting and sound equipment suitable for the touring company of "Mama Mia!" and so on, because they see every experience a student has as either enhancing or harming that student's future life course.

It's not that Camp Two patrons give the district carte blanche to spend at will. It's more that they don't need a lot of convincing about the value of the newest, latest, and greatest. They are the first to see problems (even if they aren't really there), because the way their schools look *reflects on them.*

Camp Three people are a mostly dispassionate bunch that tends to fall somewhere in the middle. If Camps One and Two are dominated by ideologues on either end of the spending spectrum, these folks are the practical members of the patron community.

They tend to absorb the information that interests them from whatever the school district disseminates and then make a decision based on their personal value equations. In other words, they approach facility issues in a very practical—rather than emotional—way. If what the district says makes sense to them, they'll support it. If not, they'll say "no."

It would be clean and simple if all of your patrons fit neatly into just one of these three camps. Unfortunately, every district has a meaningful number of patrons in *each* group. This situation creates real turmoil when it comes to communicating about building quality and its impact on student achievement, and on staff satisfaction and retention.

As such, our research suggests that moderation in communicating about facilities is the path to successfully connecting with a broad cross-section of your patrons.

This means that unless you are an *uber*district—where facilities showing even a modest bit of wear and tear simply aren't tolerated—a steady diet of information about how buildings are used and cared for is the way to connect with what matters to your typical patrons.

Messages about how you are maximizing the useful life of your buildings through seemingly banal steps, like replacing lighting fixtures with higher efficiency models, changing to more environmentally friendly cleaning solvents, and replacing flooring that is worn with material that will last longer, will build up over time in the minds of your patrons. Your district will be seen as efficient and sensible.

You should also take steps to let patrons know early and often about the changes that you envision will need to take place in your building inventory. As you do, you can't go wrong using words like "functional," "appropriately sized," and "effectively designed," because these words evoke images of fiscal responsibility, mixed with images of buildings that work well for students, teachers, staff, and parents.

It's OK to say that a building under consideration will be "nice" and "up-to-date," as long as you also put that attractiveness in the context of being able to deliver a quality education. Niceness for its own sake generally doesn't fly, except in the most upper-crust districts.

If you find yourself needing to add what many patrons consider an "audience-specific" facility or upgrade, such as a natatorium, PAC, weight room, stadium, artificial turf, and so on, our research strongly suggests that most communities will need to understand the overarching benefit from such an added attraction.

In other words, who else—besides the football team—will benefit from artificial turf (and how many years of saving on fertilizer and water will it take before the investment starts paying the district back)? Will the community be able to use the pool, and when? Is the PAC just going to be used by theater types, or will there be community-focused lectures or other programs there?

And, overall, continually answer the questions "Why this?" and "Why now?" until you are blue in the face.

Patrons have said in our research that if what you are saying doesn't appear to affect them, they don't pay attention. One well-chosen story in your newsletter, or an update sent out to those who have "liked" you on Facebook, won't cut it.

This is, as they say in the business world, a long sales cycle. But, assuming that the default opinion about the district among typical patrons is positive, those same citizens will listen and come to understand the need for such a facility, if the information is slowly and consistently delivered over an extended time period.

Case in point: We worked with a district that was playing in what was, by then, a very substandard stadium, although one that offered fond memories for a town whose population had little egress (or ingress, for that matter). However, the district was losing out on opportunities to hold regional and statewide athletic events, because its football facility was not up to snuff.

So, they set about building the case for a new facility—better parking, easier access, modern restrooms and concessions, and so forth—along with a promise to retain the treasured name of the current stadium at the new location, along with the famed arch entrance that was such an important part of the current stadium's brand.

The district kept the price tag within the bounds of what a community of its size could tolerate, and politely pointed out what their neighbors had spent on their stadiums when those facilities were built, and the events they had been able to host as a result of having those stadiums.

The result was a win at the ballot box for the stadium—and for the very essential building additions and renovations that were also part of the overall bond issue proposal.

KEY POINTS

- Each school district's patron population contains individuals who abhor spending on buildings, those who consider almost any kind of spending a worthwhile investment, and those who evaluate each request on a case-by-case basis.
- Research suggests that the best approach is to deploy consistent messages that aim toward the middle of the pack—stories about efficiency steps, making good use of existing buildings and facilities, modest updates that make a big difference, and so forth.
- Introduce the need for new buildings early, and make the case slowly. Patrons aren't nearly as interested in your needs as you wish they were. Make your patrons part of the solution by sharing details one piece at a time.
- If you need facilities that are traditionally seen as being outside of a basic education (PACs, stadiums, etc.), expect a longer sales cycle to get the word out. Make the case clearly, consistently, and slowly over time.

This is how patrons think: *Show me that you are taking care of what we've already invested in first, and then carefully explain to me (over time) why you need something new and different. If I understand how this will benefit a broad range of students and—where possible—the community at large, it's much more likely that you'll have my support when you need it.*

Chapter Seven

Essential Information

Quality of Teachers

Everyone remembers their best teacher . . . and their worst.

The best teacher was the one who showed you kindness. Who made you feel important by creating an environment where you could learn. Who opened the door to a career idea that hadn't ever dawned on you before.

The worst was the one who seemed to have it in for you. Who made you feel like a number. Or, who was just punching a time clock until retirement (and you could tell).

This memory—fond or otherwise—of teachers weighs heavily on patrons' minds as they consider the merits of their own school district. In fact, our research has determined that perception of teacher performance is, in many cases, the main factor that separates quality school districts from also-rans in the minds of taxpaying constituents.

Note the key word: *perception.*

It is the rare patron who takes the time to evaluate the statistical merits of the teachers in his or her school district. Rather, patrons' "research" consists of what they see from their own children who attend classes, what they hear from neighbors, what (again, rarely) they see and hear at a board of education meeting or other official function, and what they read, hear, and see in various printed and electronic media. Mixed in there may be their own memories of student life, if they happen to live in the school district of their youth.

It's a real witch's brew, and nearly all of it is outside of the control of the district. You could have 100 percent of your teachers holding master's degrees, but let one well-connected parent start spreading a story that this teacher or that one doesn't care about his or her child, and all the statistics in the world won't matter.

That's not good, of course. But a poor perception of a district's teachers has even more dire consequences than you might think.

Specifically, our research confirms that a community's perception of overall teacher performance is as important as—and often more important than—its views on how tax dollars are spent, in determining how it will vote on district ballot issues.

You read that correctly: A patron community's *feelings* about its school district's teachers often trump facts and figures when decisions are made about which lever to flip on Election Day.

Frustrating? Of course. You know the quality, caring, compassion, and dedication of your teachers. But most of what your patrons know comes from the ever-unreliable grapevine.

What to do? Make certain that the grapevine is filled with compelling stories about your teachers, so that your patrons get to know your educators as individuals, not simply as a means to an end (navigating children from the first day of kindergarten through to high school graduation).

Specifically, patrons want to hear news such as the following:

A teacher's dedication to his or her profession

In the "old days," athletes used to take the off-season, well, off. This meant that they did little to nothing to stay in shape, and relied on a few weeks of sore muscles during their sport's version of training camp to return to playing condition.

While most people understand that that is, in fact, old-school thinking when it comes to athletes, many of those same people continue to think that teachers show up a day or two before classes begin just to staple a few things on a bulletin board, and that they leave ASAP when the final bell rings in the late spring.

Of course, nothing is further from the truth. Teachers today face challenges that couldn't have even been envisioned when most of your patrons occupied a classroom. To meet those challenges, they are constantly involved in staff development during the year, and often continue with more formal coursework during the summer or in the evenings on what is supposed to be their own time.

Such continuing education work may be routine to teachers, but we've found in our research that it's often news to patrons.

Therefore, you should regularly showcase the work being done within the district to enhance teachers' core skills, and you should also highlight those times when teachers step out on their own to learn something new and different that will benefit their work in the classroom. Detail the teacher's dedication by sharing the *who, what, when, where,* and *why* facts, and explain the real-life impact that his or her extra effort will mean to students.

One final note: Be certain to develop a good "feeder" system for finding out about such activities. Morale rises when teachers see themselves being recognized, but can plummet when someone's Herculean effort is missed, while a rather run-of-the-mill accomplishment is highly celebrated.

A teacher's innovation in the classroom

We've discovered a lot in the last generation or two about how students actually learn.

While some still absorb information the old-fashioned way (listening to a teacher lecture, reading a textbook, etc.), research has told us that some students are visual learners, others require kinesthetic triggers, some benefit from the support of paraprofessionals, and so on.

As a result, the classroom experience has changed dramatically. Some of that change is, of course, enabled by the school district through the purchase of tools and technology that allow teachers to serve students whose educational needs and learning styles are different.

But, much of the practical, day-to-day solutions come from teachers themselves, who see needs and find ways to address them.

Our research tells us that patrons want to see teachers putting such ideas to work. It fits with the patrons' notion that a teacher shouldn't just be reading the same lessons from a textbook, year after year, but should adapt his or her approach to accommodate the individual needs and challenges of the students he or she is teaching.

These stories of innovation—and the successful outcomes they are producing—make teachers the heroes, while building greater confidence among patrons in the "educational product" you are delivering.

(Once again, it's important to develop an internal network that keeps the district informed of these great innovations, so that this news can see the light of day beyond the buildings where it is taking place.)

A teacher's commitment to the lives of his or her students

Nothing is a more pleasant surprise for a student than when his or her teacher shows up at a soccer game, dance recital, or any other part of that child's non-classroom life. It shows that the teacher really cares about his or her students as individuals.

Patrons like to hear about these moments, too, because it shows teachers stepping out of the comfort zone of their classrooms. In doing so, it also helps to tear down the notion that teachers are clock-watchers who are only trying to do the bare minimum.

Even though these are "good news" stories that merit attention, it's important to strike the right balance. A newsletter or social networking site featuring only such stories could have the opposite effect, by giving the impression that teachers are *too* involved in their students' lives. It could also appear to unfairly diminish the efforts of those on your teaching staff for whom such appearances are just not something with which they would be comfortable, or that are not possible with everything else going on in their lives.

In other words, celebrate the activities of these "over-and-above" teachers *strategically*.

Unique moments in a teacher's life

In a similar vein, patrons want to hear about compelling events in the lives of teachers in your district.

Again, you need to tread lightly in this area. But stories about domestic or international adoptions, once-in-a-lifetime research trips, long-lost discoveries made by a teacher about his or her family history, and so on, can help to personalize that teacher's story and build a stronger connection with patrons.

KEY POINTS

- Patrons view teacher performance as the most important component distinguishing quality school districts from lesser ones.
- Unfortunately, these same patrons rarely rely on statistical measures to judge performance, preferring to look to their own experiences, those of their children, and what they hear from third-party sources.
- While showcasing the general quality of your teaching staff is wise, it is also important to introduce information about your teachers that builds their brand as skilled, caring professionals.
- Reports of a teacher's dedication to his or her craft, to students, and to his or her own personal development creates a picture that reinforces the message of quality that the statistics would show, if anybody actually studied such data.

This is how patrons think: *Give me reasons to believe that your teachers are quality, caring, career-oriented individuals who understand and celebrate the unique characteristics of each student.*

Chapter Eight

Essential Information

Quality of Education

If beauty is in the eye of the beholder, our research tells us that "quality of education" is an equally vexing calculation for patrons, but is extremely important in how they judge the performance of their local school district.

For some, as we discussed in the last chapter, quality is all about teachers. For others, it's about test scores. Still others assume that if the football team is winning, then, by association, the rest of the school district must be performing well also. It's a seemingly endless and difficult-to-define list of characteristics.

One thing's for certain: It is the rare patron who cares about the intricacies of such things as AYP and the other frustrating abbreviations associated with the dearly departed No Child Left Behind initiative and other government measurement tools, until, of course, the district *doesn't* meet a benchmark, and that news ends up in the media (traditional or social). Then, the default response is usually to assume the worst.

Making matters even more challenging is, of course, that you can't even pin down what *parents* expect for their children's future.

For example, some parents are disappointed when the school district is unable to get their less-than-motivated students ready to take their MCATs before moving the tassel to the other side of the cap at high school graduation. (OK, that's a little bit of an exaggeration . . . but only a little bit!)

Other parents, however, are truly just happy to be able to call their children "high school graduates." And, of course, there are plenty of other variations on the definition of "educational quality" in between those extremes.

Throw into the mix the perceptions of patrons who have no current connection with the district (having no students in their own households, and having no contact with a student through a family member or friend), and the landscape becomes even more confusing.

So, what's the best way to get out a message of educational quality that resonates with constituents who have such varied expectations? Simple repetition.

That's right, uncomplicated, patron-friendly stories that demonstrate how the district is meeting the educational needs of students, families, and the community will do a much better job of affirming the district's classroom quality than will a chart that provides statistical proof. That's what typical patrons have said in our research: show me that you are graduating kids who have a chance to succeed.

Like tossing a rock into a stream, the publication of numerical proof of competence makes a splash momentarily, but quickly fades after one or two news cycles (again, unless those numbers reveal some seriously bad news). The interest in such data is even less focused in districts that routinely succeed. The reaction is along the lines of, "Well, of course you made AYP [or whatever the measurement du jour is]. That's what you're supposed to do, isn't it?"

(At the other end of the spectrum, districts that have struggled with such statistics run a risk that these new numbers will draw additional attention to their previously less-than-stellar performances, which is equally unhelpful in building a stronger district-patron relationship. You can almost hear their patrons saying, "Well, it's about time.")

What does actually remain in the minds of patrons for an extended time period—and tells the quality story in a much better way—is news that showcases student success and teacher innovation to deliver a quality, personalized educational "product."

Our research has affirmed that patrons like to see news items such as:

Students winning contests of all types, from science fairs, to prized scholarships, to welding competitions

In the minds of patrons, student success equals district success. By showcasing a variety of student achievements, you demonstrate that the focus is on creating successful adults in whatever fields they choose to pursue.

(One caveat: One district we worked with told us, in no uncertain terms, that "our graduates do not become plumbers." That's a direct quote. In other words, this district was populated by families for whom a post-high school encounter with career and technical education would be seen as a failure for the student and for the district. While we can debate the merits of that view at another time, it does point out a need to tailor your stories of student achievement to best fit the expectations of your patrons.)

Students being recognized within their school and their district for innovative ideas

Who says all the brainpower in a district has to come from the central office or the grown-ups at the building level? Disseminating news that showcases how students are making their schools and their districts better not only shows how smart the children are, but also how wise the district is for creating an environment in which innovation is encouraged. Talk about school spirit!

Students taking on service opportunities that benefit the community

With each generation, the belief that school-sponsored (or at least "school-encouraged") demonstrations of good citizenship are vital to a well-rounded education has grown steadily. Showing students engaged in community betterment is not only a pat on the back to parents for raising such responsible kids, but it also provides a counterbalance for nonparent patrons who, rightly or wrongly, arrive at their views of your students based on the less-motivated members of your population that they encounter.

As in all things, variety is the key. So try to spotlight the small as well as the large, the unique along with the familiar. In other words, balance stories of every student who volunteers for Habitat for Humanity with someone who organized his or her classmates for a fall workday at a senior citizen's house in his or her neighborhood.

Teachers bringing subject matter to life in the classroom

Patrons of all ages recall fondly that one teacher who made a particular subject memorable, not because of the information, but because of the presentation. These are the teachers who are legendary among students, because they truly love their material and know how to reach kids of all educational styles.

Showcasing such commitment demonstrates to patrons that teachers aren't just navigating their way through the required material—they are truly dedicated to instilling a lifelong passion for learning.

The only caution (according to what we've discovered in our research) is going overboard on highlighting the "goofy." That's because there is a meaningful contingent of patrons in every district that thinks that schools stopped teaching "the three Rs" when they let students use handheld calculators in class. Representatives of the "kids today can't even make change!" crowd always make an appearance in the results of every research project we undertake.

This group needs to clearly see the *educational advantage* of having a teacher choose to dress up like Martha Washington, for example, to not think that the district is completely off the rails. It's not necessary to censor such stories; just be certain to have a good balance of lighthearted and more serious presentations.

Teachers who excel outside the classroom in ways that will positively impact what they bring *to* the classroom

Do you have a teacher who volunteers at the Boys and Girls Club? Is leading a fundraiser for a well-known (and apolitical) charity? Has become a foster parent?

Our research says that patrons want to feel that the teachers responsible for educating the community's young minds are quality people, not just effective transmitters of subject matter. That's why they feel better about the education being provided to students if they know that those responsible for it have quality pursuits outside the classroom.

It will be important to have a good network to keep an eye and ear out for such news, lest you miss something and annoy the person, for example, who is working so hard to get his or her advanced degree in Latin, in the hopes of launching a Latin program in your school district, but who doesn't get noticed. (Also, it's critical to develop a "What if?" filter to protect you from advancing stories that are political, religious, or too personal.)

Districts that take pride in their school buildings and make certain they are maintaining them effectively

While this sounds like a fairly tedious "story," it's amazing to me how much patrons connect the quality of a school building's *exterior* appearance with what they assume goes on inside. It's a bit like curb appeal in the real estate business. If the exterior says, "Blah," it doesn't matter what the interior is like: the prospective buyer won't get that far.

The issue, our research tells us, is twofold.

First, patrons have said that they will assume the worst if there are obvious needs that go without attention for an extended period of time. Wondering what those might be? Drive by each school building and see what you can see with a patron's eye—not with your eye on the budget.

Of course, there's a reason that some items are listed under "deferred maintenance"; the funds simply aren't there to do what you'd like to do. But, even so, this is still a story that patrons have said they want to hear. Everyone understands a tight budget, but what's the plan to make certain that—as much as possible—the deferred needs are cosmetic in nature only? (This is also a key salvo in the battle to gain public support for a future tax increase. Always be showing your patrons that there's a plan.)

Second, components of building maintenance that slip over into what many patrons would consider "fluff" should be approached carefully.

For example, constructing a shelter at an elementary school for students waiting for mom or dad in the drive-up lane—while claiming poverty on classroom maintenance issues—may raise a patron eyebrow or two, while also generating some interesting e-mails and public meeting comments about the frequency of precipitation in your community at school dismissal time. (I'm sure you can name at least one or two patrons right now who could be the authors of such e-mails.)

The needs and costs are far from equivalent, of course, and your PTO or PTA might have even provided some or all of the funds for that shelter. But just as you should take a look at your buildings and their grounds with a patron's eye from a negative standpoint (as in "What looks bad?"), patrons can also harshly judge amenities that seem like a waste of money.

Districts that keep current with technology that allows their students to compete for scholarships and career opportunities

Technology would seem like the ultimate no-brainer.

However, sometimes districts forget that many, many patrons grew up without any of the conveniences that are routine today in the classroom. So, the prism through which they view such purchases—and their views on the impact they make on the quality of education—is a bit different than the prism used by most of *today's* district parents.

This is not to suggest that most patrons want students to do without. On the contrary, we're well enough into the Internet era that most everyone understands that basic computer literacy is required for nearly every career these days.

What patrons have told us in our research, however, is that it riles them a bit when decisions on technology are hard to justify for the average person.

Decisions based on convenience, rather than necessity, or that could be perceived as being solely to be ahead of neighboring school districts, aren't always hard to sell. They just require more explanation as to "Why this?" and "Why now?"

In other words, show how the technology decision benefits the quality of education students receive, while limiting anything that could smack of how "cool" you think it all is.

Districts that keep patrons informed about their long-term facility needs (and why), and that give regular demonstrations of their fiscal responsibility

If you're like most school districts, most of your patrons would say that the caliber of the teaching staff is a significantly more important determinant of a district's ability to educate children than the buildings where that education takes place.

Yet school district leaders understand that functional facilities are what allow districts to attract and retain those very teachers that patrons rave about, and that create an environment for student success. When it's time to increase the building inventory or update some of the facilities, it's important to get the message out simply, consistently, and early about the *educational benefits* of such changes.

But the days of being able to rally patrons at the time of an election are effectively gone. There are just too many things that distract voters from your messages during a shortened campaign cycle. That's why delivering messages about building needs should be on the minds of district leaders 365 days a year, *even if there are no changes immediately on the horizon.*

Simple, consistent messages of fiscal prudence and long-term facility plans, sent via district communication vehicles and the local news media (if they are willing) show that you are thinking through your facility needs before they become acute.

KEY POINTS

- Patrons' active interest in a school district's "quality of education" generally has little to do with the statistics that would actually confirm that quality (at least, in a technical sense).
- In fact, most patrons pay little attention to proficiency information, AYP data, and the like—unless the statistics are unfavorable.
- Instead, the factors they consider in judging quality are primarily memories of their own experiences (if they also attended school in the district), the experiences of their own children, the experiences of the children of people they know, and what they read and absorb through various forms of media and through gossip.
- Therefore, the information that can help tell a district's quality story centers on student accomplishments, teacher commitment and enthusiasm, and effective district management practices.
- Finding and disseminating such information should be a year-round practice for school districts, because patrons will only absorb a little of the story with each exposure.

This is how patrons think: *Rather than overwhelming me with numbers that I don't necessarily understand, show me the steps you are taking to deliver a quality education and the evidence that those steps are paying off in the lives of students.*

Chapter Nine

Essential Information

Preparation of Students for the Future

If you asked the typical patron to describe the "job" of a school district in ten words or less, most would say something like, "To put children in a position to succeed."

That's it in a nutshell, isn't it? Once a student crosses that stage at graduation, to the hoots and hollers of his or her family and friends, the trappings and traditions that seemed so important during high school give way to trepidation about the future. Is that student ready for whatever college or career path he or she may choose to pursue?

Our research has told us that a school district's perceived ability to prepare a student for the next phase of his or her life is just as important to patrons as the perception of the quality of the education he or she receives while a student—but it is much harder for typical patrons to judge, *even though they aren't shy about trying to do so.*

Why is this?

While students are in school, the evidence of their success (and the district's role in that success) is readily available. Patrons who follow test scores, graduation rates, and other numerical measures have access to that data. Parents see daily evidence of what is happening, and they may bond with a teacher or two along the way during their student's educational career. The news media covers sporting events, science fairs, and the like. And, of course, the district does its best to pump out the news of its successful students and innovative programs to constituents.

However, once the last student in a household becomes an alumnus or alumna, those parents who cared so much about your district's news become garden-variety taxpayers, essentially overnight. You simply won't get their attention the way you used to, because their pipeline to tangible proof that you are "turning out great, successful students" has narrowed, if not closed down altogether.

This is not to suggest that they no longer value a quality school district once their last child is out the door.

Quite the contrary: quality becomes even more important when that school district becomes a line item on a tax bill, rather than an organization that is providing direct services to a family member.

In essence, patrons have told us in our research that "the school district had *better* be of high quality, because I'm paying for it." (Interestingly, this seems to be the case whether that tax bill is sky-high or more modest. Patrons, as a rule, expect to see proof that their money is being well spent.)

One component of that proof? Evidence that students from the district go on to be successful in whatever their next step in life may be.

The obvious first place to look for such proof is within the family.

If children follow a post–high school path that their parents deem acceptable—no matter what that path might be—then the credit given to the school district runs from nonexistent to modest acknowledgment, depending on the individual.

That's understandable, because to heap praise on the school district (survey participants have told us) would diminish the recognition of the student's hard work and the family's support. Therefore, most of the time, a successful student is seen as being *enabled* by the school district, but not much more.

Making that even more difficult to swallow is the fact that, as all school district professionals know, the expectations of parents and the skill sets of students may not always match up.

For example, if a student's abilities are more in line with a technical education, but the parents expect him or her to have to sort through Ivy League offers, then who gets the blame when Johnny or Janie doesn't make it into Harvard? More often than not, the school district gets the lion's share.

Other proof of student success after high school comes from hearing about the achievements of children whose families are within a patron's circle of acquaintances. But, understandably, a patron's level of interest in the neighbor kid's accomplishments is fleeting at best. Expecting awareness of *that child's success* to translate into greater appreciation for the district's efforts, except in an extremely macro sense, is asking too much.

All of this creates a rather challenging scenario. Patrons want to see evidence that a school district is turning out successful students, but they dismiss much of the proof that is right under their own roof (or the roofs of friends and neighbors).

It feels like a bit of a no-win situation, doesn't it? After all, the school district can put programs in place, have the latest and greatest curriculum, employ award-winning teachers, keep the technology current, and still have students who fall short of the expectations set by those who care about them.

The lesson here is a simple one: 100 percent success in this area is an illusion. Stop chasing it, and for goodness sake, stop professing this (or anything like it) as a district objective. Common sense will tell you that it's not possible, and you don't want to set yourself up as an easy target for the cynics in your patron community.

Rather, our research suggests, patrons think you should focus on how your district helps students and their parents *set and achieve meaningful educational goals* that are in keeping with the general expectations in your patron community.

It's important to dissect that last sentence to fully grasp what patrons seem to be saying in the research we've conducted:

- *Help(s) students and their parents set and achieve meaningful educational goals*: Districts need to demonstrate their understanding that each student is an individual, and then show how each one will get the attention he or she needs to discover what his or her next chapter in life holds, and how he or she can best use public education to help get there.

  They can't do it alone, of course. The district is not a factory that can just churn out successful kids without the help and support of parents and, in a larger sense, the community. This is a critical message to express early and often.
- *In keeping with the general expectations in your patron community*: Whether you have quantified it or not, you likely have a very good idea of what your patrons view as success when it comes to the results garnered by students traipsing through your hallowed halls.

  In some districts, patrons measure success based on how many students earn academic scholarships, foreign study opportunities, and the like. Patrons in other districts give the schools a gold star for performance based on high school graduation rates, because many of the parents never made it that far.

  The typical district will have some patrons from both of these camps—and a whole lot more in between—who just want the schools to open the eyes of students to the possibilities, and prepare them to take advantage of whatever might be in their futures.

That's the key to connecting with patrons on the issue of student success: understand what they expect, and let them know what you are doing to meet those expectations.

In doing so, focus your communication on information that will ring true to the greatest number of people, with an occasional reference to students who are succeeding at either far end of the spectrum.

In other words, if yours is a district where some parents have exceedingly high expectations for their students' futures, some who are just hoping their youngsters will graduate, and still others who fall in the middle, you might focus much of your communications on what you're doing to help the "typical" student succeed. This doesn't mean that you ignore the student who gets the perfect ACT score or the one who gets a scholarship to welding school. Rather, *it means that you are matching your messages about student success to your patrons' expectations.*

Don't forget to highlight the district's role in the student's achievement, when and where you can quantify it. Whenever possible, put a face on the district's involvement by highlighting a teacher, counselor, and so forth. Showcase the *people* who enable success, not the buildings or the programs. When you're competing for your patrons' attention, they're much more likely to remember a personal story than they are program details.

KEY POINTS

- Patrons may have different components to their definition of success for a school district, but they are consistent in the simple belief that schools should prepare young people for the next chapter in their lives, no matter what that might be.
- Interest in schools, naturally, fades once all students in a household have graduated, except when the tax bill arrives, of course.
- Demonstrating proof of success among current and past students requires a sound strategy that highlights the accomplishments of current students and alumni, and that fits with the community's definitions of success—be that Ivy League scholarships, high school graduation followed by potential admittance to vocational/career training, or a blend.

This is how patrons think: *Understand my expectations for students in the school district, and then show me the real-life, everyday steps you are taking to meet those expectations and turn out students who will be successful, no matter what they choose to do in life.*

Chapter Ten

Essential Information

*Ongoing Communication between
the District and Patrons*

One of the most frustrating things for school district clients of ours is when we report that their patrons have told us that they aren't getting what they need from the district in terms of regular news updates.

If you received that piece of information, what would you say?

If you're like our clients faced with that report, you would probably protest by producing a laundry list of communication tools that you employ to push news out to the masses. Chances are, that list includes newsletters from the district and the schools, voicemails, backpack fliers, announcements sent out via PTO or PTA meetings, Twitter tweets and Facebook postings, and regular news releases to the local media (or some combination thereof).

If you are, in fact, doing all that (and, perhaps, even more), it's no wonder you would be likely to throw up your hands and say, "What *else* can we do?"

The answer: *nothing*.

If you are disseminating regular information through a variety of channels that reach both parents and nonparent patrons, then the issue is not the quantity of your news, but *the way it is presented*.

Specifically, it may be one or more of the following issues:

Complexity

We routinely have to remind our school district clients that the vast majority of those patrons they are trying to reach do not eat, sleep, and breathe

43

school district information. Yet, all too often, districts communicate with an eye toward drawing the reader (listener, viewer, etc.) into *the school district's* world, rather than the other way around.

The lesson here is a simple one: if your information doesn't connect to what matters to your target audience (patrons, parents, for example), *you aren't communicating*. The sender and receiver of information have to link up for there to be true communication.

Certainly, there are patrons in your community who want to know every detail of life within your school district. You see them at each and every board of education meeting, whether they speak up or not. They are the ones who review your budget line by line, and who (when they do speak) typically focus on a nuance that you had dismissed as insignificant.

You must be ready to feed the information needs of these individuals. These are the people who truly speak your language—for better or worse.

But not everyone is like that, of course.

In fact, our research conducted for school districts prior to "financial elections" (bonds, operating levy increases, millages, and the like) suggests quite clearly that the 80 percent who never speak up really only want to know the answers to three questions about the plans on which they will be voting:

What's in the plan? (in basic terms)
What's it going to cost me? (in actual figures for their property, not this "20-cent levy increase" language that they don't understand)
Why should I vote yes? (What problem are you solving or need are you addressing with this plan?)

The zealots will need the artist's renderings, the financial charts, and all the other details. So have this information available for them to cogitate on to their heart's content.

But remember that the masses are going to want to hear the high points, so they can rapidly understand the facts that are important to them and make their voting decision accordingly. It's just another of the many topics they have to absorb in a typical day, so don't make it difficult for them. Tell them what they need to know. If they want to know more exhaustive details, they'll search for them.

This isn't to say that the mass audience that has a life beyond school district news necessarily makes snap judgments.

In fact, the most successful election campaigns recognize that a meaningful segment of voters don't make up their minds until very late (which, unfortunately, is a fact not lost on the opposition, organized or otherwise, who tend to surface in scorched-earth form the last week or ten days before an election). Therefore, a steady, repetitive stream of the key facts is critical to make the district's case.

Connection

Early in my career, I worked for a large health care system whose physicians routinely discovered things they believed to be newsworthy. It didn't take too many swings and misses with the local media to realize that science wasn't a story, unless we could show people who were benefiting.

So when a doctor or department head would finish his or her breathless explanation of why their discovery was "news," my question was always the same: "Do you have any patients who are willing to talk about this?" If not, there was nothing to sell to the media members who were putting together their story lists.

What does this example have to do with school districts? Plenty.

If your "news" doesn't clearly answer the "Why should I care?" question, then it's not going to be heard. Consider the following "news" item: the opening of a new central office building.

By their very nature, the taxes associated with constructing a new central office building are what we call a "nuisance fee," based on what patrons have told us in our research. In other words, while patrons acknowledge that the district's leadership needs a place to work, they see no obvious, direct benefit to *education* or to the community from the creation of such a structure. As such, paying for a new central office is a nuisance.

So, when the new facility is finished, what's the news angle that's going to connect with patrons? It's certainly not administrative staff members gushing over their new digs (or taking potshots at where they were before), nor is it an extensive photo tour of the new building.

To connect with the patrons, you'll need to focus your message on what this new central office means to students, parents, and the community, rather than what it means to those who will sit at the desks, tap away on the computers at those desks, and answer the phones.

Is there community meeting space? Will a new phone system associated with the new central office allow for faster service? Will access to the kinds of records needed by patrons be more streamlined?

See the difference? Instead of a palace where the staff resides, it's a hard-working, patron-focused facility.

Another example: the dreaded operating levy increase proposal.

Bond issues are sexy, because they lead to new buildings, renovated space, or something that you can point to and say, "I voted *yes* for that." This doesn't mean that bond elections are a slam dunk, of course, only that it's easier to showcase the end benefits for students, staff, parents, and the community when the funding leads to physical structures or other tangible items that you can see, touch, and tour.

Operating levy increases, on the other hand, are a different story.

From the point of view of the cynical patron, a district that asks for an operating levy increase is saying, "We want you to spend more, but (most of the time) you won't get anything new as a result. We'll just be paying our people more, and buying more stuff that we think is important."

For these patrons, there are no tires to kick, no buildings to admire, no stadiums to sit in on Friday nights. It's business as usual, but at a higher cost to them.

To make a connection with patrons on an operating levy increase, *you have to connect with what they value* and explain how your proposal protects and preserves what they cherish.

The low-hanging fruit in most districts we've worked with is teachers. As mentioned earlier, perception of teacher performance ties directly to views on the overall performance of the district itself.

Fortunately, patrons typically love the teachers, and they see them as the lifeblood of the district's work. Operating levy increases are typically spent (at least at some level) to protect or enhance staff salaries. Make that connection, and you have a message that is more meaningful to patrons than any pronouncement of how many Smart Boards you'll be able to buy with this new money.

That should be your guideline for everything you disseminate: *Am I saying how this benefits students and the community?* If not, your "news" will not connect with those you are trying to reach, making it even more likely that they will tune you out in the future.

Consistency

When I was in the advertising agency world, I once worked with a hospital client who started my first meeting with them by asking a simple question: "So, what's our fall campaign going to be about?"

This hospital had routinely spent all its marketing money in the third and fourth quarter (with a different agency, I might add) and just randomly picked a different specialty or service area to feature each year. The ads looked different, the tagline never stayed the same, and even the logo sometimes got a "sprucing up."

The result was that those who worked in the section of the hospital that was being featured (and the physicians associated with that section) were delighted. But the needle never moved in terms of utilization. So the ads had been a failure.

What went wrong? Well, it wasn't the creative, which, while it wouldn't have won any national awards, was solid for the midsized market where it was playing. It wasn't the placement—the city had one newspaper that everyone read (remember those days?), two radio stations, and a scant few billboards, and that's where they had always placed the advertising. Even the money being spent was suitable for the marketplace.

What it lacked was consistency. There was nothing to tie the advertising together from year to year, so those in their target audience—who weren't nearly as interested in the advertising as the hospital was—had to work extra hard to figure out each year who the sponsoring organization was when the ads hit in the fall. They had solid creative, but no consistent look and feel that linked the messages about the Sleep Center from one year with those about the hospital's new cardiac surgery capabilities the next year, for example.

This quest to always be talking about something new can bedevil school districts as well, when patrons just want to hear regular updates on the aspects of school district life that they find most important.

So while you may get extremely bored with stories about how green your new building is, which teacher won a statewide award, or how a particular graduate is excelling in his or her career, our research suggests quite strongly that this is what your patrons are most passionate about.

Go ahead and throw in the occasional story about how the new track surface is easier on the athletes' joints or about what the school board learned at the statewide convention. Just remember that your patrons appreciate a steady stream of updates on how you're spending their money, what's new in the classroom, and how you are turning out great students who will become productive members of society.

If you look hard enough, you can easily keep the flow of those stories going. You just have to resist the temptation to think, "Haven't we said *enough* about this already?"

The answer, consistently and simply, is *no*.

KEY POINTS

- Patrons will frustrate you when they say, "The school district never tells me what's going on," even though you can produce a mountain of evidence to the contrary.
- It's important to recognize that it's not the volume of information you disseminate that matters, but whether or not it's important to those you are targeting.
- Avoid complexity. Most in your audience will want a simple presentation of the details that matter most to them—tax dollars, teacher performance, and so forth—so resist the temptation to force-feed every nuance to every patron (although you should have those details at the ready for those who are interested).
- Make certain your news connects with what's important to your patrons, not what's important to you.

- Be consistent. Resist the temptation to routinely stray from the list of what's important to patrons that appears on the Patron Information Pyramid, just because you have become bored. In fact, remember that most patrons pay little attention to *anything* you say, which is why you have to focus your message, and say it over and over again.

This is how patrons think: *Realize that schools are one part of my busy life. Keep me posted primarily on what I've told you I'm most interested in, while making more detailed information available, too, for those times when I want to learn more.*

Chapter Eleven

The Middle Tier of the Pyramid

Important Information

Below the top level of the Patron Information Pyramid is a set of topics that generally don't achieve the same level of interest among typical patrons as those in the "Essential" category.

Note the key word in that sentence: *generally*.

This means that you may look at the list of topics in the "important information" category and see one or two items that always seem to come up in conversation, whenever you encounter a group of patrons.

Take class sizes, for example.

The class sizes of my generation would be scandalous today in many districts. I went to suburban, middle-class schools, and it was not at all uncommon to find thirty students in an elementary classroom managed by a single teacher—without the help of a relatively new invention, the paraprofessional educator.

My parents didn't concern themselves with how many students were jammed into my classroom. That was something the district would decide, they figured. (They were more interested in what my report card said.)

To them, there was little relationship between class sizes and the quality of education. If the teacher was good, he or she could handle more kids.

However, many of today's parents shudder at the thought of classes that are two-thirds as large as Mrs. Stewart's third-grade class in 1967 at Katherine Carpenter Elementary School in Overland Park, Kansas.

Research (and common sense) has proven the value of more one-on-one attention from teachers, and school districts have used this information to feed patron thinking when it comes to pushing for an operating levy increase that will help maintain class sizes that are considered suitable in today's world. The result: parents and patrons are more sensitized to the slightest movement in average class sizes than they would have been a generation or two ago.

This means that, in some districts, the leadership must continually bang the drum with class-size information, because patrons expect it. In others, where there may be large groups of "It was good enough for me; it's good enough for them" patrons, class sizes may be the same afterthought it was to my parents.

All of this is to say that placing these items in the middle part of the pyramid was a judgment call, based on the average of all the research studies we have conducted since 1992.

But it may not be completely accurate for your district. You may need to nudge class sizes, or some other topic we placed in the middle group, up or down, because it is more routinely on the minds of your patrons than would be the overall average for that issue. As I said earlier, the formula is not cast in stone, but should be taken as a guide.

Not only can your district have a topic that always would be above or below the middle level on the Pyramid, but you can have movement that is somewhat more episodic in nature. There is no better example of that than the topic of "student safety," which we'll discuss in more detail later.

For most districts, it's generally a nonissue. But that doesn't mean that there aren't situations that cause a flare-up of interest. It just takes one well-publicized skirmish on a bus, incident between students after hours in the school parking lot, or story about the bullying policy not really making a dent in the problem to catapult it from "important" to "essential," at least temporarily, in the minds of patrons. (Add the unfortunate national headlines of recent years to the mix, and even districts with a spotless safety record can find themselves on a temporary high alert about this issue.)

In the same manner, an extended period of peace and quiet—sort of like those signs posted at job sites that say "This site has had 105 days without a lost time accident"—or if it's just never a problem in your district, could move the issue from "important" to "as needed" in terms of your communication priorities.

All of this is to say that our goal in calling the items that follow "important information" is to find the most logical spot for these topics for the *average* school district, based on what patrons have told us.

As you consider whether the middle of the Pyramid is the right spot for these issues in your district, it will be important to bring some balance into your mental review of what patrons have told you.

In other words, treat it the same way figure skating is scored (without the scandals): Toss out the high and low scores, then add up and average what you hear in the middle to come to a judgment. Then, communicate accordingly. The ideas shared here on these subjects will fit, no matter where you place the topic on your own personal district Pyramid.

Chapter Twelve

Important Information

Performance of Principals

The importance of spending time communicating with your total patron audience about the work and success of your building principals is the first of several topics in the middle section of the Pyramid that you should evaluate with a real "fork-in-the-road" mentality.

Specifically, your current parents will have a much more significant interest in principals and their roles in keeping school buildings running smoothly, because smooth-functioning buildings contribute to student success.

However, those patrons who have no children, or who no longer have children in your schools due to graduation or because they have transferred to a private or home-school setting, will have almost no interest. After all, why should they?

That's why this topic finds its way into the middle of the Patron Information Pyramid. Information about these key professionals must be strategically identified and advanced, because there are large groups at both ends of the interest spectrum, when it comes to principals.

Look at it this way: Our research suggests that typical patrons see principals a bit like the store manager at their favorite retail establishment. They know someone is in charge, but they base their overall impression of the store on the quality and appeal of the merchandise on the shelves and on the helpfulness of the staff when a need or question arises.

Substitute "school" for "store," and it's easy to see how patrons can and do make the comparison. Most patrons instinctively drill down to the classroom level, and judge a school's quality based on their perception of the teachers and the educational "product" being delivered to students. The principal is there to oversee things, but tends to be a rather nebulous figure for typical patrons.

Parents, on the other hand, have a somewhat clearer image of the principal at a school that their child attends. They know his or her name, and—particularly in the younger grades—often have a relationship with him or her, driven by the parents' desire to maximize the school experience for their child. Even so, the principal is often seen by typical parents as a manager who holds (and attends) a lot of meetings and who occasionally is called on to make a disciplinary decision, but who mostly has the responsibility to keep the ship sailing in the right direction.

Where the principals tend to get the most credit is for the environment they encourage—or mandate—in the school building.

The principal sets the tone and expects staff and students to follow his or her lead. This can be practical, in the case of having a strong antibullying stand, for example, or it can be more social, such as standing out in front and greeting students every day as they arrive for class.

When the environment is less positive, our research suggests that patrons tend to heap more blame on the principal than on anyone else employed by the district. Interestingly, patron comments we see in our research on topics such as student behavior run much more toward "They need to make those kids behave," than toward "Students should know that they need to behave in school."

Again, who takes the fall? Typically, it's the principal, for allowing an environment to exist in which such behavior lapses are tolerated. Like the baseball team that fires the manager, because you can't fire all the ballplayers when things are going poorly, the default for patrons is to question the leadership. (In all fairness, patrons often lump the *district* leadership and the board of education into the mix when issues like this surface. File this under the category of "Who's running that district, anyway?")

This dynamic creates an interesting challenge when it comes to communicating about the work and wisdom of principals, because parents already have at least some sense of the contributions of these professionals (albeit a somewhat limited one), while those without a current direct connection to the district typically pay attention only when the news is negative.

Therefore, our research suggests that the best options to promote the excellence of your principals are as follows:

Focus on principals as enablers of student excellence.

Students succeed because teachers are committed. Teachers are put in a position to succeed by principals who create the expectation of excellence and who build an environment where such a high level of performance is possible.

That's a message that can tie the work and commitment of principals to the performance of students in a school building and, of course, to district-wide success.

But be careful how you advance this message. You don't want to unintentionally downplay the fact that it is the classroom teachers who make it happen on a day-to-day basis. Better to make the principal a "head coach" or even, sometimes, a cheerleader of sorts, championing the work of his or her teachers and their students. If there is a specific program or approach that the principal has instituted, focus on that. But the safe bet is to position the principal as almost like a proud parent of both teachers and students.

Focus on principals as professionals seeking to grow their own skills.

As mentioned earlier in this book, your patrons may or may not know (or assume) that teachers participate in continuing education of some form. But that part of a principal's existence is, according to our research, foreign to them. Focusing on what a principal has done to expand his or her skill set is a good story to relate for two reasons.

First, it serves to encourage and celebrate the achievements of principals, and that builds greater camaraderie within a district's leadership team. Any chance to make middle managers—which is what principals really are—feel valued should be maximized.

Second, our research shows, over and over again, that a district's brand mostly lives and dies based on what happens at the building level. As such, showcasing professional advancements that are taking place, if you will, at the point of service delivery (the school) says that building-level personnel are valued and that their continued growth and development is respected.

The equation is a simple one in the minds of patrons that we have talked to: *Even if I'm not completely sure what they do, I know that better principals create better school environments, where strong teachers can thrive and students can succeed.*

While you don't want to try to draw the attention of patrons to every continuing education conference a principal attends, important milestones make a compelling case for excellence, and will catch the eye of those watching your district's performance.

Draw attention to principals who build a real sense of community within their schools.

This is a bit of a subset of being an "enabler of excellence."

As mentioned above, the enabler story is one in which the principal creates an environment in which excellence is expected and championed. That story defines how principals have created a healthy, nurturing environment, in which students, families, and staff are truly a team whose members would do nearly anything for each other.

Each district has schools in which the principal is so beloved that any conversation about moving him or her elsewhere in the district is met with outrage. In those cases, he or she is not an employee of the district; he or she is "*our* principal."

There is no one story format on this topic, because every principal approaches this challenge differently. But if there is a strong sense of community, this will really be seen as a celebration for families who are in that community, and as a spirit-filled story of dedication for others.

Be careful in how you approach this, however. In telling this story, you need to focus on the evidence of community, and introduce the principal's role with a logical amount of attention.

In other words, the story is, "Anytown Elementary families pull together to better their school, says Principal Smith," rather than "Principal Smith is beloved by all." (That later story is fine, however, if Principal Smith is retiring!)

The distinction is that Principal Smith is seen as part of the team that makes this feeling of community possible; he or she is not the sole cause. That allows you to tell this great story without appearing to separate, for special attention, one principal over another—a situation that will bring about unwanted ripples throughout the district. The school is the story; the principal helps make it possible.

KEY POINTS

- The interest level in the activity of principals varies greatly. Current parents are interested to some extent; past parents and "never" parents rarely think about principals.
- In general, typical patrons see principals as managers of the schools where they work. As such, if the school is running smoothly, the principal fades into the background. If not, they are thrust into a glaring spotlight.
- Focus your communication about principals on how they enable excellence in their buildings, what they are doing to make themselves better principals (and, therefore, create even stronger schools), and how they are part of building a great sense of community at the schools where they work.

This is how patrons think: *If the school is running smoothly and the students are succeeding, I'll assume that the principal is doing a good job. If you have a story to share about his or her work, use it to help me understand how a principal can impact excellence.*

Chapter Thirteen

Important Information

Student Safety

Early on in our work with schools, I had the opportunity to conduct focus groups for a district that had gone through a cultural and socioeconomic evolution over a couple of generations.

Back in the day, as they say, this district was considered an oasis that attracted blue-collar individuals who were fleeing the neighboring big-city school district, but who didn't have the resources to flee all the way to the suburbs—if they even had the desire to do so.

The result was that while the district had some ethnic diversity, the balance was definitely tilted toward working-class whites. They lived in neighborhoods full of hard-working people, in what would be considered "starter homes" if they were located in the suburban communities adjacent to the district. For these patrons, however, it was home. It felt comfortable and safe, and it would always feel that way. Or so they thought.

Then the district began to see a slow, but worrisome, decline in its student population. This time, people *were* leaving for the suburbs (at least, ones they could afford). These were not upward relocations. Rather, these citizens were leaving to find places where the neighborhoods (and, though very few would admit it, the neighbors) resembled how things *used* to be in our client district.

The assignment we were given by the district was to figure out if the patrons' perception was that the changing ethnic and socioeconomic mix had made their schools unsafe.

Make no mistake, the district *had* seen an increase in incidents of student violence over time, and the administration had deftly handled the fallout from each one (when there was any such fallout) with the news media, staff, and parents. In real numbers, the district was hardly turning into a modern-day "West Side Story." But it was the only reason that the school board and administrative team could come up with for the patrons' flight.

And they were right. While the district was safer—in terms of the actual number of incidents—than most of its blue-collar, multiethnic neighbors, the *perception* was that it had become more dangerous, due to the changing characteristics of its student community.

Therein lies the rub when it comes to the issue of student safety; it's a topic that you'd really prefer not to touch. But in many districts, it's one that you can't avoid. Add in the national headlines about school violence that have caused our nation to grieve, and the communication issues at the local level expand exponentially— beyond the typical local perils that used to be all that parents had to worry about.

As you would expect, patrons have told us that they expect their schools to make a commitment to provide a safe environment. To them, it's like paying the light bill; it's a nonnegotiable item.

So, when a district makes a big fuss over its "safe environment," patrons wonder what is really being said. Among the choices:

"We feel the need to tell you this, because some people have said we aren't safe." (Or, "Because of the national headlines, we're concerned that you might panic.")

"We used to be unsafe, but now we're crawling with resource officers who keep the troublemakers in check."

"We're safer than district X, so why would you want your kids to go there?"

"That incident you heard about was really no big deal."

Take your pick, and then add to it the things you may have already heard about your own district.

Student safety is a double-edged sword issue. If you bring it up, most patrons will wonder why. If you don't—and you make the news because of a safety-related situation—you will find yourself in a defensive posture that you likely don't deserve.

Making matters worse are two realities that weren't in place when most of your patrons were in public school.

First, safety in the time when your patrons were wandering the hallways of their own schools generally meant making certain that after-school scuffles and other types of miscreant behavior were kept to a minimum. Today's safety issues—as we know all too well—have the possibility of much more devastating consequences than the fistfights of a generation ago, and are happening more often in schools full of what the media would call "good kids." The result: it doesn't matter where you live; safety is always on the minds of students, staff, parents, and the community.

Second, technology has created a whole new, difficult-to-manage venue, where safety issues can crop up unnoticed by school leadership. From gossip spread on social networking sites, to sexting (the unwanted sharing of supposedly private photos with a broader network—often in retaliation over a broken relationship), and all manner of misuse in between, students can bully each other from a distance these days, creating a beneath-the-surface challenge.

So, in such an environment, what's the best way to communicate with patrons the message that the community's offspring (which may include their own) are learning in a safe environment?

Focus on what your students are accomplishing.

If students are succeeding, their environment is geared to enable that success. That means an environment populated by great teachers, challenging curriculum, a great effort on the part of the students themselves, and a feeling of safety and security.

This isn't to say that students can't succeed in school environments where safety is more of a concern; thousands of them do so every day. It's just that successful schools are *assumed to be safer* than unsuccessful schools—so our research with patrons tells us.

So take advantage of that assumption by pushing your students and their stories of success into the limelight.

In the same manner, celebrate your teachers.

The intent is the same, but the example is different. Great teachers work in great (thriving, encouraging, and safe) schools.

The proof is in research that we've done after a district has failed a bond issue (or failed it again, or for a third time, etc.). Invariably, the teachers in those districts score high marks for their performance in the minds of typical patrons.

If that's the case, then the school district—or, more likely, the campaign committee—has a message platform: You want to keep these teachers you have said are so great? Then put them in buildings where they can continue to thrive.

In one instance, we worked with a district that had failed a bond issue for a badly needed new high school five times in a row. Think about that for a minute. Five times. You want to be the one to try and get volunteers for campaign committee number six?

The new high school (which would replace the decaying current campus) was to be built in a newer, more thriving part of the community, and would have all the security bells and whistles that were crudely retrofitted at the current facility. (Of course, the new high school would also have many more curricular and facility advantages.)

What we discovered in our research for the district is that the teachers were extremely well thought of, but the district had made a strategic error by only engaging community volunteers to get out the story of the ballot proposal. Teachers were active participants on the committee for try number six, and could talk—during their off-hours, of course—about the classroom and safety advantages of a new facility.

While teacher involvement in the campaign wasn't the only factor in the ballot box win, having them step up and help make the case changed the tone of the conversation.

It doesn't always work, of course, but this example showed how it can elevate the decision beyond purely bricks and mortar (and cost). Now, patrons can put a human face on the changes, and on what might happen if they aren't supportive at the ballot box.

If the equation works for great teachers needing to work in modern—or at least adequate—facilities, then it also works for them needing to work in safe places. Show stories of happy, successful teachers, and patrons will immediately connect that happiness to the environment. After all, it's hard to be happy if you don't feel safe.

Showcase steps you are taking to maintain a safe environment.

Safety in a school setting has always focused on preparedness. After all, students learned how to "duck and cover" during the Cold War, and fire and tornado drills in schools are as standard as grilled cheese and chicken nuggets in the cafeteria at lunchtime.

In recent years, of course, additional drills to keep students safe in the event of an unwanted visitor have been added to the mix, and schools are renovating their facilities and making procedural changes that make it extremely difficult for anyone to enter their buildings unannounced.

These are good, sensible updates that are in keeping with the times, so there's nothing wrong with highlighting the common sense precautions you are taking. Keep your rhetoric in check, however. Patrons have told us they want to see that these steps are logical parts of a plan to *maintain safety*—not to "make the kids safe."

Personalize your resource officers.

A "police presence" in school used to mean that the building had been beset by so many troublemakers that the law was finally summoned. Now, even in the most upper-crust districts, resource officers have become just another member of the team (albeit a member with a very different responsibility than a math teacher).

The best way to diminish patrons' concerns about "Why school X needs a *police officer* in the building" is to let these staff members speak for themselves—with a little guidance, of course. Even in schools where they have some "officering" to do on a regular basis, the focus should be on how they seek to bond with students, and how in doing so, they can spot and solve issues before they become problems.

KEY POINTS

- Student safety concerns are not limited to school districts where safety has, in fact, been an issue. Changing demographics and the perceptions often associated with those changes can make it more of a front-and-center topic.
- In communicating about your commitment to safety, reinforce the successes that are happening in your schools—for teachers and students—because success is more likely to happen in a safe environment that enables it.
- Don't shy away from talking about enhancements to your security systems and drawing attention to your resource officers, but make certain to focus on how these steps (and these people) are part of a plan to *keep* students safe—not *make* students safe.

This is how patrons think: *I expect you to provide a safe environment. Demonstrate your efforts in that area in a variety of ways—not all of them actually having to do with safety—and my image of your schools as safe places to learn will be enhanced.*

Chapter Fourteen

Important Information

Class Sizes

As I mentioned earlier, class sizes are a real "eye-of-the-beholder" issue.

You likely have a segment of patrons for whom class sizes were substantially larger during their school careers than yours are today. To them, what's a few extra kids? After all, isn't that why you hire great teachers—to handle the needs of a lot of kids?

Most of your current parents, of course, are at the other end of the discussion. Our research tells us that many of them have in their minds what they *believe* is the ideal number of students for their son's or daughter's class (or classes).

For some, it's an eyeball situation, as in "Wow, this class *looks* rather crowded/busy/hard to manage." For others, they've done some homework, checked the web for the latest research, and have a number in mind. And, they're not at all shy about sharing it. With you. At your board of education meeting. At the local pie and coffee house. You know these folks well.

In our planning process leading up to patron research for school districts that are considering a ballot issue, we tell our clients that we have found the issue of class sizes to be the ultimate trump card.

If the district is having no luck getting people to support the new facilities that a bond issue would fund, having an alarming rating on "class sizes" in our research results is like a gift from above.

Why? Because it gives the district the right to say, "You told us that you were concerned about class sizes. This proposal will solve that."

(Of course, if the data says that patrons find class sizes to be a non-issue, the proposal's merits would have to be broader than simply more elbow room for students.)

Unfortunately, one other constant is that it's impossible to create a profile of the kind of district whose patrons would be most likely to be concerned about class sizes.

In other words, if you are thinking that the patrons who fuss about classes of more than twenty are only in well-to-do districts, think again. Our experience is that demographic characteristics and socioeconomic status have no consistent bearing on patron opinion on this issue.

Specifically, we worked with one less-than-wealthy district, where the average elementary class size was fourteen—that's right, fourteen—and patrons expressed concern in our research that the classes were too large. Another district with a similar economic profile and a more typical class count gave the issue only a scant mention.

(Interestingly, patrons in the district in which classrooms seemed too full at fourteen students also gave their teachers more modest grades, compared to those given to teachers in the other district. The teachers weren't lambasted; they were just not as adored as they are in the majority of districts where we work. So the issue here seemed to be more a concern about the performance of teachers, masquerading as a concern about class sizes.)

In essence, the only sure thing we can tell from our research is that patrons assume that overcrowded classrooms—*based on however they would define that*—make for a less-than-quality school experience.

Your question, of course, is "OK, so what do *our* patrons think about our class sizes? Do they think we're overcrowded?"

Ideally, this topic should be part of routine patron research you conduct. It's the only way to be certain that you are hearing from a true cross-section of typical patrons, not just the ones who fill up your voicemail, e-mail, and the chairs in your board meeting room.

But between the times when formal research is conducted, you should put your principals and teachers on assignment to be listening and reporting on parent opinions on the subject, and you should place your administrative team on high alert for patron comments.

Also, check social media networks, blogs, and even comments attached to the end of stories on your local media websites.

While all of these are unscientific approaches, they will provide you a glimpse into patron opinion trends on this topic. (You should track these things at all times, not just for class-size feedback. In doing so, however, it's important to keep a cool head. These sources tend to be populated by the overly passionate, not by a true cross-section of your patrons. In other words, be sure to have some antacid at the ready.)

If this reconnaissance suggests that you need to address the issue, stay as far away as possible from promoting the latest *scientific* studies on class size, which show the limited impact of one (or two, or three) more students in a classroom, or anything like it. This may be good information for educators. But if you share it with your patrons, all you will do is

- create a concern on this issue among those patrons who, until you spoke up, thought your class sizes were acceptable; or
- cause those who had the concern initially to dig their heels in even further.

Instead, our research suggests that it's best to approach this in the same way you would approach student safety, by focusing on success in the classroom.

Specifically:

Draw attention to typical students who are succeeding.

All too often, patrons will tell us in our research that "the school district has programs for students who excel and for those who struggle. But it's the ones in the middle who get left behind."

Reading between the lines, the message is clear: *my school district doesn't care about "average" kids.*

And, of course, patrons reason, it's easier to "get lost" and be underserved by teachers if the class sizes are larger than (they think) they should be.

So, while it's always good for the district to draw attention to the students who get the perfect ACT scores, or to the ones getting scholarships, or to those who are being offered a chance to study in Europe for the summer, don't leave out the students who have to grind it out every day to be a success.

Your district has many more of these students than it has superstars, and promoting their accomplishments will showcase the fact that the more typically successful student is being well cared for.

Introduce your patrons to those on your staff who help to minimize the impact of larger class sizes (paraprofessionals and such).

Patrons who worry about class sizes are often looking at simply the raw number, as in "How many students are in this classroom?" What they miss in that rudimentary headcount, of course, is the impact of paraprofessionals and others whose presence eases the burden on a teacher.

(In a way, paraprofessionals are a bit like the physician's assistants who are popping up in larger medical offices. These trained professionals are qualified to handle basic care needs and tend to be more accessible than the doctor. The result is more flexibility for the doctor, and greater access to care for patients.)

By and large, patrons don't fully grasp the impact of paraprofessionals on the atmosphere and productivity in a classroom, because most of them were never exposed to such staff members in their school experiences. Enlighten them, and it will help tell your district's story of excellence.

Detail your efforts to provide appropriate class sizes for different age groups.

Any patron who has sat in a college lecture hall listening to a professor pontificate on his or her subject matter is familiar with the fact that class sizes increase as students become more mature.

Not only is it more fiscally prudent to do so, but the more mature a student is, the more his or her school experience should be like the real world, where you have to advocate for yourself, rather than rely on a doting teacher to see how you are doing.

This isn't to say that you should suggest that crowded high school class-rooms, for example, are ideal. But the typical patron will be much more amenable to the idea of larger upper-division classes than he or she will with the mental image of rows and rows of tiny desks and chairs crowding an elementary school classroom. Don't ignore this opportunity to show how you are working to mitigate the effects of larger classes by being strategic (where you are able) in where you allow them.

KEY POINTS

- Class sizes have become much more of an issue for this generation than they were when the parents of your current students were in public school themselves. Competing studies about the impact of class sizes don't do school districts any favors, because what's suitable in one study is too large in another.
- Patron research can tell you whether it's only the squeaky wheels who are concerned about class sizes, or if it's a commonly held concern.
- If you find that class sizes and/or "overcrowding" are issues for your patrons, this becomes a strong plank of any informational campaign for a ballot issue to alleviate that situation. After all, "You said that class sizes were a concern. This bond issue addresses that problem" is a powerful argument for your proposal.
- You can lessen the worry about class sizes by drawing attention to stu-dents who are succeeding (with no mention of class sizes—just highlight your successful students), by showcasing paraprofessionals and others whose presence helps to diminish the impact of larger classes, and by

explaining how you are making decisions about class sizes in an effort to minimize their impact as much as possible.

This is how patrons think: *I want my child to get individual attention, and I'm concerned that larger class sizes will make that impossible. Show me what you are doing to keep class sizes down, and to maintain the quality of education, particularly if you have no alternative but to increase the number of students in each classroom.*

Chapter Fifteen

Important Information

Technology Available to Students in the Classroom

One of the most fascinating constants we have found in our research for school districts emerges when we ask questions about what would fall under the general category of "the classroom experience."

These questions generally include asking patrons to rate a district's performance on teaching "the basics" (English, social studies, math, and science); on preparing students for success in life; on helping students develop key life skills, such as problem solving and communication; and on the technology that districts have at each student's disposal.

No matter how they feel about the other issues, there is a near-universal view among patrons that up-to-date technology is essential for success in school and — more importantly — in life.

The number of research participants who lament that "kids rely on computers too much . . . back in my day . . ." is declining rapidly. For the most part, patrons recognize that technology plays an important role in the classroom today, because it is ubiquitous in society.

Where these results are not as consistent, however, is on what constitutes "up-to-date technology" in the eyes of patrons. It can vary greatly district by district, school by school, and even grade level by grade level.

Patron opinions run from those who whine that their kindergarten student has to share a laptop with another child in school, to those who wonder where all the books are in what they still quaintly call "the library."

Then, of course, there is the problem of obsolescence. While the magic of leasing versus buying helps address this issue, most school districts—including yours, I would imagine—have a variety of ages of hardware and, perhaps, software populating your buildings. Chances are there will still be some students using technology that is meaningfully older than that being used by other students.

In thinking about communications on this topic, it's critical to remember the 80/20 rule from earlier, but with a bit of a twist. In this case, recognize that the 20 percent of patrons who are passionate on this topic will always think you are behind the curve and that their children will fail miserably in their future careers if they don't have unfettered access to the latest iPad at school, for example.

You will never be able to satisfy them (and you will also find yourself in a battle you can't win between fans of competing products), so don't fight it. Answer their questions and address their concerns when they come up, but resist the temptation to try to prove how right your approach is.

Instead, direct your communications to the 80 percent who just want to be confident that their school district understands the important role technology plays in student success, and, therefore, has a plan to keep such tools updated. If you feed them a steady diet of easy-to-understand updates on your technology accomplishments, they will have their needs on this topic satisfied.

For example:

If you have a school that switches from a computer lab to a computer cart that travels from room to room, highlight the benefits. Mobile computer carts mean less unproductive time for students getting to and from the computer lab, plus the transition time to get refocused, and so on.

If you negotiate a deal that provides routine upgrades to your student-based technology—and you are able to bring the price down from the previous arrangement—that's news to share on two fronts (cost-efficiency and better technology).

If you have success with a one-to-one laptop initiative in which students are allowed to take their laptops home at night (and you have a year without theft, loss, or damage, for example), you can tout the responsibility of your students, and the fact that this initiative is making their homework time more productive.

When you switch from wired to wireless in all your buildings, you can highlight the advantages of the greater flexibility that comes with a wireless environment.

And so on.

As you think about informing patrons about the technology you have available for students, keep two constants in mind:

First, keep the "technology side" of your story—meaning the gory details—limited, so that someone with a more rudimentary knowledge of the subject matter can understand it.

This is important, because you want a cross-section of your patrons to actually understand what you are saying, and you don't want to be so complex that your cynics might say "Sounds mighty fancy . . . wonder what *that's* costing me?"

In other words, for example, don't describe how the wireless network was structured or even how it works, but rather the benefits that will result from this change.

Second, with extremely rare exception, you should focus the story exclusively on how students (rather than staff) will benefit from the technology enhancement.

If there's a teacher side to the story, find a way to make the benefit to teachers connect somehow to the benefit to students.

For example, if you sign that deal for routine updates, like the one mentioned above, you can talk about the obvious benefits to students of staying current, while also highlighting any tutorials or training your staff will receive, so they can "help students make the most of this upgrade."

If, however, the benefit is exclusively at the district level, think twice before promoting this news, unless there's a significant cost savings, or the upgrade will speed up service to patrons, and so forth. Otherwise, it will come off to some patrons that "the district office is bragging about its new computers!"

Another aspect to consider as you evaluate promotion of the technology available to students is to think about how your district stacks up to other districts in your region. There are potential pitfalls in promoting your status on technology, whether you are the leader, you are average, or you are woefully behind your neighbors.

For example, if you routinely have the latest and greatest, such technology in the classroom has become expected. So a lot of fanfare about a computer upgrade will seem like a waste of time to those in the know, and will get those who may not be as aware wondering just how far behind the district was. (The answer may be "Not behind at all!" But you don't want to plant any seeds of doubt.)

If you are somewhere in the middle of the group, then the tightrope you are walking is balancing the news about your upgrade with the knowledge held by some of your patrons that, "X School District *still* has better equipment for students than ours does."

And, of course, if you are way behind, you can almost hear patrons say a collective "Finally!" when it comes to the news of a technology enhancement.

Make no mistake: Keeping students connected to the tools they need to compete in the global economy *is* news. Just be certain that you think strategically about how you keep your patrons informed, rather than simply touting your latest technology bell or whistle.

KEY POINTS

- Technology has become recognized by all but the most curmudgeonly patrons as a key tool for students in a twenty-first-century classroom.
- Even so, there will be disagreements among patrons about what constitutes the best technology choice. This is an argument you will not win, so don't get involved.
- Instead, focus your presentations on the district's efforts to maintain current technology for students and how the changes will benefit the learning experience. Think of benefits such as speed, efficiency, greater opportunities, and so on.
- Keep the information simple enough that a typical patron can understand it, without having to have an IT professional standing by to explain.
- Consider where your news places your district in comparison to other neighboring districts, and present your information accordingly.

This is how patrons think: *Keep student technology current. Explain your decisions in terms that I can understand, and in ways that allow me to see the benefit to students, not simply as something that will offer the district greater cachet.*

Chapter Sixteen

Important Information

District Promises Made and Fulfilled

"But we *told them* we'd be back to them to ask for another bond issue to fund the projects in Phase III of our long-range facility plan," said the district superintendent. "Why are they saying now, in the research, that they don't remember anything about that?"

Because they don't.

Our research with school districts can confirm, beyond a reasonable doubt, that patrons' memories are what we like to call "long and foggy."

They're "long" when it comes to remembering minute details of a slight visited upon them by a staff member, when all they wanted was a copy of their child's transcript mailed to six different colleges the same day of the request. Or a teacher who made middle school math a nightmare for their Johnny or Janey. Or an offhand comment by a school board member about a school that "might be closing" (someday).

On those topics, they've got the memory of an elephant—at least according to what children's books would have us believe about the intellectual capabilities of your nearest pachyderm.

Where they get "foggy" is on the nuts and bolts of how districts make decisions, the fact that you can't use the funds from the bond issue they just passed to pay your teachers, or that your long-range facility plan calls for a ballot proposal to build another middle school in five years.

Where this really hits home is when patrons "misremember" (as the politicians like to say) a promise they believe was made, and take out their frustration over this supposed failure on the offending school district.

Case in point: We provided research services for a school district that had—in the minds of their leadership—made it crystal clear that its long-range plan called for the district to eventually expand and renovate its middle school, and then to have the high school and middle school swap buildings.

At the time they debuted this plan, patrons either voiced their strong approval, nodded in general support, or didn't say anything. And merrily along the district went, assuming that it had received approval for taking this step when the time was right.

Well, *ten years later*, they went to the voters and said, "Remember when we told you that, one day, we'd be back with a ballot issue to fund this expansion and school-switch plan? Now's the time."

You can guess what happened. The measure lost, rather soundly.

Our research, after the fact, revealed that patrons claimed to have no recollection of this plan, and thought that the district's leadership had gone a bit off the rails in proposing something the citizens considered rather bizarre.

Cue the conversation at the beginning of this chapter . . .

Make no mistake: The district did the due diligence when it introduced the plan.

Where it slipped up was in expecting patrons to be as interested in (and as focused on) the long-range facility plan as the district's leadership, board of education, and staff members.

Add in the wrinkle of ten years between the presentation and this election, and it's no wonder that what seemed to district leaders like the next step in an agreed-upon process turned so sour at the ballot box.

So, what's the lesson here? Actually, there are three.

First, recognize that your patrons have a limited attention span, so you should communicate detailed plans and promises accordingly.

As I mentioned earlier in the book, 20 percent of your patrons will likely read your long-range facility plan—10 percent to "ooh" and "aah," and 10 percent looking for a negative "aha!" they can point out to you. The rest won't pay attention to anything more than the high points, if that.

Remembering this fact of life, prepare for the needs of the 20 percent by loading up the details on your website. But give the masses the facts and figures they need and want, in "What-does-this-mean-to-me?"-sized nuggets.

This means that you don't talk to the 80 percent about a "carefully integrated plan that will create appropriate learning spaces for students to progress into their futures as the district's student population expands and the current facilities are no longer suitable." Rather, you say that the plan "prepares the district for when new schools or renovations will be necessary to keep class sizes ideal for students and staff."

While most promises that get school districts into trouble have to do with facility plans, the same guideline applies to promises related to long-term discussions about taxes, curriculum development, extracurricular activities, and the like. Always be thinking, "What would a typical patron want (or need) to know about this?" and plan your communications accordingly.

Second, keep your plans and promises on the "outer edge" of the patrons' radar at all times.

Where our client district that was described above erred was in thinking that the discussion on its plan had taken place once (and, I might add, very effectively at the time), and therefore it could be shelved until it was time to field the bond issue. That was expecting way too much from patrons.

Instead, find opportunities to keep reminding patrons about key components of any plans and promises your district has made. Drop them into newsletter stories and web copy. Insert a mention into a parent letter. Have your parent organizations bring it up here and there with the punctuation "and, as you remember, this is part of the district's long-range facility plan" (or something similar).

Don't overwhelm; just make it one part of the ongoing district-patron conversation.

Third, as you complete components of a plan or a promise, say so.

One of the biggest mistakes a district can make is assuming that patrons will see a puzzle piece dropped into place and remember what the entire picture looks like. When district officials expect this sort of "oh yeah, this is all part of *the plan*" memory, they are naturally bewildered when district patrons begin to complain about a step in that plan.

While it may, at first, seem a bit childish to say, essentially, "Remember when we told you that we were going to do X, because it was part of Y? Well, we did. W came before. Z is next. . . ," each time a step is completed, it's critical to helping patrons remember that you made a promise and that you are fulfilling it.

There's no need to be dramatic; matter-of-fact language should be your style, because while you may approach the debut of a plan with fanfare, the completion of individual steps are just the next chapter in the story.

KEY POINTS

- Patrons have little difficulty remembering a slight they were dealt by their local school district, but most of them have less interest in committing to memory detailed plans or extensive promises from the district that involve multiple steps, an extended time period, or both.
- The majority of patrons also have little interest in committing to memory such basic facts of school district life as how bond funds may and may not be used. This can create frustration for school district officials, who, when they get the same questions from patrons time and again, say to themselves, "But, we've *already made this clear.*"
- The best solution is to find ways to keep a steady drumbeat going regarding plans and progress—what's happened in the past, what's happening now, what will happen in the future. Assume that each patron receiving the communication is hearing it for the first time. This will help ensure that the messages stay simple.
- As steps in a promise or plan are completed, say so. Do not be shy about reminding people—in a business-like manner—that what you are reporting is a promise that was made (and the fact that you are reporting on it means that it's a promise you've kept).

This is how patrons think: *I'm too busy to remember complex plans and details. The only way for me to track anything this detailed is for you to break it down for me into small pieces. Each time you have something to say, make it simple: what you did, why you did it, and what I might have forgotten from the past that ties to what you are telling me now. And, above all, don't forget to tell me why I should pay attention.*

Chapter Seventeen

Important Information

Spending Balance

If there was ever a topic that is a perfect example of the potential inaccuracy of settling on an "average score" among a wide range of responses to a question, patrons' views on the balance of spending between academics, athletics, and other extracurricular activities would be it.

Simply put, if you haven't seen more than the odd e-mail gripe or heard the random snide comment from a patron here or there, it's not an issue at all for your school district.

But if there's a steady refrain of "Why do we have so many football coaches?" or "Why are we spending money on activities [or facilities] that have nothing to do with reading and/or writing and/or arithmetic?" then you have a problem.

There really is no middle ground. (Although with such a wide range of opinions, there really is no other place for this topic in the Pyramid than in the middle!)

In districts where the issue of spending balance is a problem, it tends to really make itself known when it comes time to put a ballot issue before voters that has something "extracurricular" on it.

As mentioned earlier, bond issue projects that seem to be focused only on a specific segment of students tend to rile up those patrons who already think that the district spends too much on "frills." If those feelings are strong enough, they can sink a ballot issue all by themselves, regardless of what the rest of the projects look like.

Case in point: We tested the waters for a school district on a bond issue which—if all the component parts found favor with the patrons in the research—would have been the largest bond issue in the history of the school district's home state at that point. So a lot was on the table.

Sensing that including the construction of another stadium might put the whole proposal at risk, we did something rather creative in how we structured the research. Specifically, we asked about all the components *except* the stadium first, and found that support for that proposal was a solid 60 percent. Because this district was in a simple-majority state, that was great news. Then we said, "Well, what if the proposal also included an additional stadium?" (There was more to the question than that, but you get the drift.)

Support for the same proposal—just with the addition of a new stadium— dropped to 38 percent. The district saved the stadium for another day, and won the election. (And it made certain to tell patrons throughout the initial campaign, "We heard you. No stadium.")

What's interesting about this example of fussing over how the money is spent is that it comes from a very well-to-do district, which, I assume, goes without saying if we're talking about the potential of *another* stadium. But it could just as easily have come from a district that has much fewer resources and needs to replace a running track that had become dangerous, some seats in its auditorium, or some stadium lights that are from another era.

By the same token, districts whose patrons don't seem to have any concerns about how the resources are divided between books and basketballs also defy easy definition. They aren't always the districts whose high schools win state football championships, for example, or those who have little to no extracurricular options (whether by choice or by budget).

To determine where your district stands on this issue requires research that is no more scientific than keeping your eyes and ears open. See what your patrons are saying, and read what they are writing. Check in with your parent group leaders. Watch the membership levels in your booster clubs, and track the patterns.

If you discover you have a potential problem with how your spending balance is perceived, here are some steps to take.

First, expand the story beyond the obvious.

Patrons who only see synthetic turf at a stadium as benefiting big, burly football players six or seven times a year are missing the utility of such a surface for other groups, such as the band, and for routine PE classes, for example. Regularly reminding patrons that so-called frills have multiple applications is critical.

Second, give as much attention to the accomplishments of your debate team as you do your basketball team.

One of the rubs for those who dislike school districts spending money on sports is that it takes funds away from pursuits that are more cerebral than physical. Your district can alleviate at least some of these concerns by showering praise on your debate team, your musical performers, and so on.

Third, focus attention on clubs and other activities.

While the funding side of such activities is downright paltry in comparison to the funding for sports, showcasing the work of students involved in community service helps to tell the entire story of how your students are spending time away from the classroom, under district supervision. It's also a dynamite reinforcement that your district cares about all students, no matter what their 40-yard dash times might be.

Fourth, accept reality—you won't please everyone.

Set a plan for how you will allocate funds to extracurricular activities. Listen to your patrons. Update the plan as necessary. But don't let the patron who regularly harangues you via e-mail sway you—because once you satisfy his or her demands, he or she will simply be replaced by someone else.

KEY POINTS

- In some districts, the balance of spending between academics, athletics, and other extracurricular activities is a huge issue. In others, it barely registers.
- If yours is a district where there is a concern, the chances are good that patrons believe that too much—rather than too little—is being spent on extracurricular activities (usually sports).
- To address this concern, expand the story of your extracurricular activities to show how more students benefit than might be expected. (Synthetic turf opens up the football field for band practice and other activities, for example.)
- Also, focus attention on non-sports-related extracurricular activities and clubs, to demonstrate the district's well-rounded approach to providing an environment for student growth and achievement.

- Above all, recognize that you won't be able to please everyone. So have a plan, and adhere to it.

This is how patrons think: *Show me that you are applying common sense to how you divide funds between the classroom and the playing field, and don't forget to celebrate the accomplishments of those whose exploits do not involve wearing the uniform of their school.*

Chapter Eighteen

The Bottom Tier of the Pyramid

As-Needed Information

The bottom level of the Patron Information Pyramid consists of those topics that, our research tells us, are not of much interest to the typical patron until there's truly something meaningful to report.

The issue here is to understand the difference between what's meaningful to *you*, the school district, and what passes that same test for a patron population that runs the gamut from your active "frequent flyer" parents who are on every committee, down to those folks who only think about the school district as they grumble about their tax bills.

So before you invest resources and make a play for the typical patron's attention with something found on this level of the Pyramid, consider the following:

1. Is it a time-sensitive story, or is it what journalists typically call "evergreen" (meaning that there's nothing special about it today that wouldn't be just as special next week or next month)?

   If it's evergreen, it might not even *be* news. But stories that announce date-specific accomplishments by students, key votes by the board of education, or the arrival of a new superintendent qualify as news, because they won't be stories a few days after they happen.

2. Is there a "patron impact" component to the story, or is it just the district tooting its horn, or reporting on something that the average person would likely find rather tepid?

   If you can't pinpoint a reason that typical patrons—again, try to think of both ends of the spectrum, plus that gigantic group in the middle—would be interested in, it's not worth the effort.

3. Will patrons likely be posting, tweeting, or blogging about this issue, or in any way discussing it?

Sometimes, stories that don't really pass the test of being news-worthy still have just enough of a question mark about them that they might start tongues wagging in your district. In such cases, you need to get ahead of them by making certain your news is out there.

Here are some examples to put a real-life spin on the above guidelines:

Your board of education having its monthly meeting *is not* a story. Your board of education voting at its monthly meeting to place a bond issue on the ballot *is* a story.

Your high school football team starting practice *is not* a story (except in the most rabid communities). Your high school football team having two players who ran an Alex's Lemonade Stand over the summer to raise money for cancer research *is* a story.

Hiring a new assistant for the superintendent *is not* a story. Your superintendent's assistant having written a book about her experiences in public education *is* a story. (Hopefully, it's a funny, complimentary book!)

See the difference?

If it only matters to you, it's not a story.

Chapter Nineteen

As-Needed Information

Extracurricular Activities

Our research suggests, quite strongly, that the level of interest in the extra-curricular activities of a school district (or, more appropriately, of schools within a district and/or the student participants from those schools) is driven primarily by demographic characteristics.

Certainly, those whose children are participating (along with a subset of other parents whose children attend the same school) would qualify as pa-trons who are interested in most anything that has to do with their offspring's sports teams, musical performances, drama, debate—you name it.

And if you live in a *community* that truly fits the definition of that word, then there might be some merit in considering active promotion of your extracurricular activities.

The test to determine if you are such a community is as follows: are your high school football games the talk of the town, so much so that your stadium is packed with townies, seniors (meaning older adults in this case, rather than about-to-graduate students), and families with kids who aren't anywhere near high school age? If you answered *yes*, then you qualify.

Another test: If the potential addition of synthetic turf to your football field will actually help your bond issue pass—rather than put it at risk—you also qualify.

Otherwise, there's very little likelihood that information about most of your extracurricular activities would be considered newsworthy.

This means that you shouldn't spend a lot of time trying to find ways to get the local media to run stories about your upcoming staging of *Brigadoon* in the high school PAC. It simply isn't news to typical patrons, and those who are already interested in such fare can (and will) find out about it through internal channels.

Now, there is one caveat to this counsel, and it involves what could loosely be defined as your "public display space."

Specifically, while there is no value in using your financial and human resources to try to stimulate publicity for the aforementioned staging of *Brigadoon*, there's a subtle public relations benefit to posting a notice about the upcoming performances.

So, for example, news about the event—including pictures of the rehearsals, if you think they are of suitable quality—should certainly find a place on your district website and on the website of the school where the production is taking place.

The performance dates, times, and other details should be noted in any electronic or written communication that you routinely send to parents and nonparent patrons. Outdoor marquees at the school (if you have them) should post the key details. And, if you really want to get promotional, you might consider hanging a banner above the school entrance touting the upcoming performances.

Will this stimulate a meaningful jump in attendance? It might among the students and their parents, but don't expect much from the community at large.

After all, unless it involves their own children, their children's friends, or the children of one of their family members or close friends, can you really see many people in your community saying, "You know what, honey? Smith High School is staging *Brigadoon* tonight. I really like that show. We should go!"?

No, probably not.

But that shouldn't be your goal. Rather, you should see these tactics as a way of demonstrating to the taxpaying community that your school (and your district) is providing a well-rounded education to individuals with all types of interests, and that it's an engaging place to be a student.

Again, focus primarily on using your existing communications tools to promote the facts and figures about extracurricular events outside of sports, and you'll enjoy some added recognition for the school in question and for the district as well.

Sports, of course, are another story.

Your local media, in whatever form it takes, is often more than happy to cover the exploits of your primary revenue sports—typically football and boys' basketball at the high school level. You might also be fortunate enough to have media that still do the occasional features on other sports, particularly when it's state tournament time.

For this reason, it's likely unnecessary to put much district effort into promoting your sports programs and the athletes who compete therein. It's already news in your community, and your booster clubs will likely fill in the gaps.

If, however, you find yourself with a student athlete who has a unique story to tell that goes beyond his or her exploits on the field of play, you should consider it.

Outstanding academic performance (a perfect ACT score, for example), a commitment to community service, leadership in school clubs, and so on, are all good stories to tell, and they give you the opportunity to say, "You may know John Smith for his game-breaking runs down the football field. But did you also know that he spends his weekends after football season building houses for Habitat for Humanity?"

Think of it a bit like the Olympic athlete profiles that are offered during the television coverage every two years. We already know that these athletes are fearless on the luge, have a floor exercise routine that is pure ballet, or are so fast on the track that you expect to see animated "speed lines" behind them. What makes these profiles magical is that they tell the rest of the athlete's story.

Use those Olympic athlete profiles as your model, because these are the types of stories that might not be covered if you didn't unearth them for the media and that, like the publicity regarding your arts-style extracurricular activities, provide further evidence that your school district is producing good citizens, along with good students.

Let the media tell the obvious stories themselves, without any work from you (except for providing them the information they need). You concentrate on keeping a low but steady drumbeat on everything else, using the easiest available communications channels.

KEY POINTS

- Unless yours is a community that lives and breathes high school football or some other sport, the likelihood of there being significant, systemic interest within your community about your complete menu of extracurricular activities is small.

- However there's nothing wrong with using the space and venues you have available to promote your extracurricular activities—as long as you recognize that it will drive awareness that you serve students with a variety of interests and talents, but will not likely drive much in the way of additional attendance.
- Update your website with pictures of students preparing for plays, musical performances, debate competitions, and such. Use your outdoor marquees, and consider banners, if appropriate, to spread the word.
- Let your local media and booster clubs promote your sports programs, although you can feature athletes for other aspects that make them unique—volunteerism, starring in the classroom, and so on.

This is how patrons think: *If you're going to communicate about extracurricular activities, tell me a story beyond the obvious. Show me a different side. Help me get to know more about the people involved, beyond their exploits on the field, on the stage, or in the competition.*

Chapter Twenty

As-Needed Information

*Courtesy and Responsiveness of Staff Members
(In Schools or in the Central Office)*

The idea of a school district actively communicating about its success in being courteous and responsive to the needs of patrons reminds me of an encounter I had very early in my career, while assisting a small-town hospital in Missouri with its communication activities.

The hospital was completing what, for them, was a major renovation. It would bring the institution out of what was known as the Hill-Burton era, a period in which rather rudimentary hospital facilities were constructed across the country, so that health care could be nearer to everyone.

The hospital public relations director with whom I was working was taking me on a tour of the upgraded facility, which was almost complete (bathrooms in every room now, for example), and she pointed with pride to a glass divider that separated the lobby from the office where patients checked out and reviewed their bills. Etched on that glass were the hospital's logo and the words "We care."

My immediate thought (although I kept it to myself, being thirty years junior to the public relations person) was, "You're a hospital. *That's your job*. What's so unique about that?"

Our research demonstrates that school district patrons feel pretty much the same way when it comes to the issue of courtesy. They give a district and its personnel (usually at the building level) no credit for doing what they consider to be a key part of their jobs, but they remember the slightest shortcoming in this area.

What this usually means is that we see three groups of people in our research results.

The smallest group is patrons who have suffered through some demonstration of poor service, and they are more than happy to pinpoint, in chapter-and-verse detail, exactly what happened and, usually, who was at fault.

In fact, reviewing the detailed descriptions in our telephone surveys of slights committed toward patrons by supposedly uncaring staff members helps to break up the monotony of numerical calculations when we're analyzing research data. Some of the stories people tell show just how long their memories are when they feel snubbed. (Remind me to tell you sometime about the school secretary I keep reading about in our research results who "never passes along my messages to the principal!")

The mid-sized group consists of patrons who give the school district good marks for courtesy and responsiveness, either because they have actually experienced a high level of service themselves, or they feel so good about the district overall that they're willing to just assume the best in this area.

In most districts, however, the largest group—by a landslide—consists of people who say "don't know," when we ask them to rate the district's performance in the area of courtesy.

This shouldn't come as a surprise, in that the majority of families in most school districts do not have a current student in the household. While it's true that patrons in our research are usually not shy about offering their opinions on a lot of areas about which they currently have no personal knowledge, the courtesy and responsiveness of school personnel seems to be where they draw the line, throw up their hands, and profess ignorance.

Therefore, there's no real benefit to be gained by trying to drum up interest in what most patrons believe are simply routine parts of a staff member's job description: be nice, answer questions, and solve problems. Doing so gets you no pats on the back. Promoting that you do so only gives some of your more critical patrons a chance to opine that you are only touting your courtesy and responsiveness because it's been an issue in the past.

In fact, you should only promote your staff's courtesy and responsiveness if you have a story to tell that patrons don't already know, and that you think would help build the school district's brand. Think "human interest."

If a staff member helped expedite a student's enrollment so that the student's father could be involved before he was shipped overseas in the military, that's a story.

If a staff member answers a call, realizes a patron is having a medical emergency, and summons help, that's a story.

If a staff member has a reputation for being the person to be counted on when homemade baked goods are needed for a PTO meeting, that's a story.

It's not staff members doing their jobs that's a worthwhile story; it's staff members doing *more* than their jobs in the areas of courtesy and responsiveness. That's a story that, if told effectively, is probably worth the effort now and then.

KEY POINTS

- Most patrons simply assume that your staff members will be courteous and helpful, while smaller groups may have had negative or positive experiences that stand out in their memories.
- Because being courteous and helpful is expected and assumed, there's little to be gained by spending resources seeking to occupy patron "brain space" with stories of your staff members fulfilling this responsibility.
- However, if a staff member's courtesy has an unusual twist, consider featuring him or her, under the strategic thought of "look at all you get for your tax money."

This is how patrons think: *I expect district and school staff to be courteous and to address my needs, because I pay their salaries through my taxes. If there's a human interest angle, where their service made something good happen that's above and beyond the expected, I might want to hear more about it. But be selective, because my bar on what's "above and beyond" is set pretty high.*

Chapter Twenty-One

As-Needed Information

Performance of the Superintendent and the Board of Education

The research results are in, and the findings are consistent from district to district: unless there's a *negative* reason to pay attention to the superintendent and/or the board of education, typical patrons simply assume that all is well.

More so than with any other category of evaluation questions we ask in our patron research studies, having a high percentage of participants saying "don't know" on the topics of the performance of the superintendent and the board is the research equivalent of death and taxes: it's pretty much a sure thing.

(The reaction we get from these school leaders to this lack of awareness of their efforts ranges from relief to utter disappointment. We always try to guide those who are disappointed back to planet Earth. The measure of a superintendent and a school board is not how much they get noticed, but how much they get done. Leave the "getting noticed" to teachers, staff, and students.)

Think for a moment about the last news story you saw about a superintendent or a school board. What was it about? Chances are good that it wasn't positive news.

Arguments at board meetings. Heated disputes about the budget. Questions about whether or not the superintendent should be retained. Board candidates taking the district to task on all sorts of issues. And, if you're really unfortunate, news about inappropriate behavior—professional or personal—on the part of the superintendent or a board member, that has set tongues to wagging across the district.

For example, we worked with a district that used our research results to affirm for their board that their bond issue lost badly, because two of their board of education members campaigned actively against it—*after* joining hands with their fellow board members to vote *yes* to authorize the election. That's the kind of story that shoves a school board and its district into the spotlight for all the wrong reasons.

On the positive side, you might get the random story about a superintendent getting an award, or the board being named the School Board of the Year, or something along those lines. But those are rare occurrences, and they generate little, if any, interest among typical patrons. In most school districts, it's just not news that board members attended a conference to get better at their volunteer jobs, or that the superintendent has another plaque on his or her wall.

The risk in such a situation—in which the news typically only surfaces when it's more negative than positive—is that the school district will step up its communications in an effort to achieve more balance (almost like a journalistic antidote to less-than-stellar news). The advice from patrons through our research is simple: don't bother.

There's no real benefit to a school district if their superintendent or school board members have a higher profile. Making a concerted effort to make this happen runs the risk of distracting your patrons and of wasting the limited attention they give you.

This isn't to suggest that you won't find yourselves having to *respond* to certain stories, rumors, and assorted gossip about the superintendent and board of education, and their activities, at some point. These individuals are community leaders, and so their actions are going to be scrutinized by the local media, as well as by gadflies who make it their obsession to watch public officials like hawks. Chances are, you have some of these types of individuals who regularly attend board meetings, so you already know who they are.

But responding is different than actively disseminating news.

Active dissemination of news about the superintendent could make him or her look like a publicity hound, and patrons tell us that that doesn't sit well with them.

Pushing out news about the board or its members crosses a rather delicate boundary that shouldn't be crossed. After all, the board of education is the body elected by the community to lead its school district. If the school district does too much to promote the individuals who are supposed to be, if you will, the community's watchdogs *over* the district, it could send an unintended message that the board members may have an overly casual approach to their duties. Promote an individual member of the board, and you run an even greater risk of seeming to try to curry favor.

See how this can quickly turn good intentions into a slippery slope? For the most part, there's a general assumption among patrons that these individuals are performing their duties, expressed in the form of a high percentage of "don't know" responses. It's just not on your patrons' radar screens. Take that news as a blessing.

KEY POINTS

- Patron awareness of the performance of school boards and superintendents is typically low—unless that performance is the subject of scrutiny by the media. Such routine disinterest should be seen as good news.
- When there is scrutiny, it's wise to be prepared to respond. But trying to stir up interest in the activities of school district leaders is often counterproductive.
- If the focus is on the success of students and staff, the board and superintendent will be seen as contributors to that success.

This is how patrons think: *If you try to get my attention by aggressively promoting the board and/or the superintendent, I'll wonder why. My interest is mostly in the teachers, students, principals, and individual school buildings. Unless you give me reason to wonder if all is well, that will be my assumption.*

Chapter Twenty-Two

Special Situations

Handling Hot Topics

In 1988, as Oldsmobile was beginning its long death spiral, the brand's advertising agency tried to distance the nameplate from its long-standing stodgy image by saying that the new Cutlass Supreme was "not your father's Oldsmobile." The television spots showed young drivers in a car with an up-to-date design, rocked an upbeat music track, and displayed that car zipping around appealing scenery. The spots generated buzz, and the slogan even became part of our national chatter for a while.

But the effort only delayed the inevitable. The brand founded in 1897 could not escape its image of practicality. It was an image that had been lovingly crafted and that had made the brand a success in a different era, but it ended up as a straightjacket from which the brand could not escape when the preferences of car buyers changed. And in December 2000, General Motors announced its plans to discontinue the Oldsmobile line.

Public school districts face a similar challenge in helping patrons of all ages understand how the reality of today's educational environment differs—both positively and negatively—from what it was like yesterday.

You think the gadget industry (cell phones, tablet computers, etc.) has a corner on obsolescence? Take a look around your district, and make a list of what's new, different, hot, and not-so-hot compared to a year or two ago in the same classrooms. Go ahead and write on the back of the page if you need to.

Now, take that ever-changing landscape and add to the mix the following patrons, many of whom belong to more than one of these groups:

- The "Get Back to Basics" crew: These are individuals who believe, among other things, that students stopped being able to do math once calculators were introduced into the classroom.
- The "Have You Seen What They Are Doing in Europe?" group: These are folks who are constantly scouring the web for information about other educational approaches, the importance of class sizes, and other components of "the latest research."
- The "I Remember When" team: A close cousin to the "Get Back to Basics" folks, these individuals don't want to hear about how diverse the student body is today, in terms of socioeconomic status, access to suitable food and clothing, and varying language skills, or about how that diversity impacts the ability of students to learn and teachers to teach.
- The "Statistics Don't Lie" crew: These folks want to measure everything, and believe that teachers, school districts, and students can be effectively judged through a single evaluation. (Their polar-opposite cousins are, of course, the individuals who believe that schools only "teach to the test" these days.)
- The "Can You Send Me an E-mail About That?" team: These are the individuals who appear only at parent-teacher conferences or when an issue surfaces that merits their attention. Their disconnection (except when it is convenient) makes it difficult to make them a part of their student's educational team.
- The "Question Everything" patrol: You know these individuals well, because they are the first to say they will "vote *no* on anything the school district proposes until they cut all the waste" and that "the school district has to start operating like a household; when there's less money you need to cut back."

That's just a start. You can probably identify an additional audience or two that is unique to your school district.

To this confusing cast of characters, you must regularly introduce, explain, defend, and/or celebrate the latest educational strategies, trends, and tactics that are impacting life in the classroom and at the district level—knowing that each person will judge the merits of your information using the prism through which they view schools and, candidly, all of life.

So what is a school district to do? Here is our counsel about explaining complex topics, drawn from our patron research.

First, keep it simple, and tell me why I should care.

Patrons tell us, quite clearly, that their school district's level of fascination with the details of the latest and greatest in education far exceeds theirs. If you bury them in facts, figures, charts, and graphs, trying to get them to match your enthusiasm, the overwhelming majority will quickly tune you out, making your job more difficult when you have updates to share on the same topic.

Second, tell me what this means to students.

Use benefit language that crisply pinpoints how life is about to change (hopefully for the better) for students. Stay light on the blocking-and-tackling aspects of the changes, except in cases where process details are necessary to explain the benefits.

Third, tell me what it means to other key stakeholders.

Think about teachers, parents, building-level administrators, and the community at large. Focus on the "need to know" information that helps to define the change or changes clearly for your patrons.

Fourth, tell me how this connects (or doesn't connect) with other trends, practices, or findings.

But, again, keep it simple.

Fifth, point me to other resources for more information, if I am interested.

The order here isn't random; it's critical. Simplicity should always be the watchword when trying to detail the merits of such trends as Twenty-First Century Learning Skills, class-size management, and allowing personal electronic devices in the classroom.

Flash back, for a moment, to the Patron Information Pyramid in the front of the book. Picture the same shape, but apply it to the expected level of interest that a cross-section of your patrons will have in learning more about the latest hot topic.

You'll draw the attention of the most people if you keep it simple. Somewhat fewer numbers of people will also want to know what this means to students. Still fewer people will also care about the impact on other stakeholders, and so on.

The smallest group of people consists of those who will want all the details. Those people will be very satisfied if you place these minutiae in a designated spot on your website.

If you keep this variation on the Patron Information Pyramid in mind at all times, you greatly increase your chances of connecting with each patron at a level that piques the maximum interest possible from him or her on the hot topic at hand.

With that communications approach as the foundation, here are some thoughts about how it might be applied to a few topics that are likely to remain hot for quite some time. (This is not intended to be a complete list, as hot topics do change. But you will easily notice a common theme throughout the counsel provided here that will continue to hold true when the "next greatest thing" comes along.)

Common Core

While all your patrons have likely heard about Common Core through the news media, the subject runs the risk of being easily as perplexing as No Child Left Behind, which baffled most people with all its nomenclature (AYP, subgroups, etc.). On top of that, you can paste the nuances of "a government program," "teaching to the test," and "failing schools," and you have a real witch's brew at work here, from a communications standpoint.

To steer clear of that steaming cauldron, focus your primary communications on the key benefits, while loading up your website with all the ins and outs. Those benefits, from the perspective of patrons, are as follows:

First, Common Core is focused on mathematics and English Language Arts, which are the building blocks of education. If ever there was raw meat to satisfy the "back to basics" crowd, this is it. Telling patrons that Common Core is designed to ensure proficiency in these foundational subjects is a great start to explaining the benefits. Even those who don't view education quite that narrowly will have a hard time arguing with a focus on math and English.

Second, Common Core provides a more uniform method of measuring skills in earlier grades, so that individualized attention, if necessary, can be called into action sooner, rather than later. It's important to demonstrate that the regimentation associated with Common Core is benefit-driven—students with needs are identified earlier.

Third, parents, community leaders, and teachers played a role in creating the standards. While this won't completely appease the "it's a government program" crowd, it's still a valuable message to deliver.

Fourth, the standards set a foundation from which students can and will grow. It's important to help patrons steer clear of the notion that the standards create *limits*, when, in fact, what they really do is set minimums. Focusing on how the standards make certain that all students have the basics needed to pursue their dreams creates the proper context for understanding them.

Class-size debates

If you want to sponsor a debate comparing web research on this topic versus personal experience, get a set of current district parents and people of grandparent age together for a conversation.

Current parents who have a bone to pick about class sizes can usually produce reams of data as to why your district's class sizes exceed the ideal, while those from older generations can equally regale you with stories of grade-school classrooms, back in the day, with thirty or thirty-five students—one or two of whom were even troublemakers—and yet the teacher "did just fine."

If you are asked to wade into that discussion, recognize that comparing your class sizes to the guidelines set by your state's Department of Education has a bit of an "Oh yeah? Says you!" quality about it.

Instead, aim for a middle ground. Patrons want to hear that you take this issue seriously, and that you are monitoring the situation, so that "class sizes do not impact our students' opportunity to learn."

Doing so not only shows your concern, but also creates a powerful dynamic when your growth necessitates a ballot issue for more facilities. If you wait until the need is painfully evident, your sudden attention to the topic will cause suspicion. If you are regularly monitoring the situation (and reporting on that monitoring, as necessary), your ballot request becomes the next chapter in an ongoing story.

International comparisons, year-round school, online options, and other nontraditional approaches

In most districts, the classroom dynamics and the approaches to teaching employed today bear only a modest resemblance to those in practice just a few years ago. Go back a generation, and the comparisons become even more difficult.

While the education model in which teachers present material at the front of a classroom remains a staple in many buildings (and, candidly, a preference for many teachers), there's so much that's exciting and newsworthy that's taking place in classrooms that doesn't involve a lecture.

Capturing those improvements effectively for patrons requires a focus on benefits first, and style second.

In other words, recognize that your patrons have lived through changes in curriculum, teaching styles, and classroom organization their entire lives. In fact, I'm old enough to remember when team-teaching was the hot trend, and the so-called new math was actually new!

Where public schools lost their way on presenting information about these topics in the past was by using an "inside-out" approach. In other words (using the same example), rather than talking about "how much more rapidly students will master math facts with what has been dubbed 'new' math," they tended to drone on about "what's different in how we're teaching math today."

Patrons, on the other hand, lead with benefits when they want to talk about alternative approaches to traditional classrooms. They tout studies about how students in Finland are ahead of the pack, how more classroom time that comes with year-round school will make our students more competitive, and how retention of material absorbed through online media is higher than traditional lectures, and so on. Benefits first, process second.

When presented with questions, comments, or suggestions on how to recast the school experience, districts should take two important steps.

First, demonstrate an open mind. You may have no immediate plans to convert to the Finnish school model or any other idea advanced by a patron who has done his or her research, but one look around your district will tell you that things are far from static. Just look at the explosion of Career and Technical Education programs. Show of hands: ten years ago, how many of you thought you'd see, for example, large-scale culinary programs in high schools across the United States?

Second, follow the patrons' lead, and focus on benefits first. A former coworker once told me that those in a particular target audience didn't want an answer to the "What?" question; they wanted an answer to the "So what?" question. When you need to explain something new, in terms of the classroom, always lead with the "So what?" followed by a brief presentation of the "What?"

Use of technology in the classroom (one-to-one initiatives, allowing students to use personal electronic devices in the classroom, etc.)

Because they are easy to get one's arms around, all the various "technology in the classroom" stories are often used by school districts seeking to look up-to-date. One word: *caution.*

A patron doesn't have to be old-school or a penny pincher to start wondering, "Why do all those kids need iPads?"

Don't add to their anxiety by focusing on the equipment. Instead, position the equipment as an *enabler of education* that is better, faster, more focused on today's world—whatever description or descriptions you prefer.

Initiatives that put devices into students' hands mean less down time, more opportunities to investigate, and more chances to identify creative solutions to problems. It's not about gifting a computer to a student; it's about not letting a lack of available technology hold students back.

Recognize that your patrons may not know the difference between, for example, the latest version of an iPad and the previous one, but they do have at least a passing knowledge of what a tablet computer looks like and does. Therefore, they will really only want to know what your students will do with the ones the district is providing.

Impact of a more diverse student socioeconomic profile/closing the achievement gap

One of the hottest, and touchiest, topics a school district has to address is the evolution of its student population and the challenges that greater socioeconomic diversity can create in the classroom.

It's likely that a larger percentage of your students than ever before come from homes where English is not the primary language. Where at least one parent is absent. Where food and clothing are not as plentiful as they are in other households.

It's an endless list of challenging personal situations that school districts did not create, but with which they must deal every day. In almost every district, teachers find themselves with one eye on the curriculum and the other on the status of the health and well-being of their students.

This situation creates an unfortunately hot topic having to do with the impact that students with greater personal challenges and academic needs may or may not have on other students, and on the district as a whole. And those with a slightly more altruistic view of this situation would also like to see how the district is working to close the achievement gap between the highest-performing and the most-challenged students.

On an issue as complicated as this, the information needs of parents are different from those of non-parent patrons, according to our research findings. (And, believe me, the subject comes up in districts of all shapes and sizes—not just in *uber*districts where the expectations for student achievement are sky high).

In our research, parents have said that they feel better about their school district when the district talks to them about the success of its students of all academic skill levels. Finding opportunities to celebrate results gives a district many avenues to showcase its efforts to serve the needs of all students.

Non-parent patrons, on the other hand, tell us that they are typically less interested in the details and more interested in evidence that the district is protecting its brand. Whether they have dreams of selling their home in the near future and thus have purely monetary reasons for wanting quality schools, or they simply have pride in their community and want to see one of its foundational elements protected, demonstrating the success of students of all academic levels will accomplish that.

The best solution: Stake out a position as a district that believes that all students can achieve success, and then demonstrate specific ways you are enabling, encouraging, and extracting the maximum possible achievement from each member of your student body. Document the details on your website, and focus primarily on the headlines that give both parents and non-parent patrons something they can easily digest.

Teacher evaluations

As mentioned throughout this book, typical patrons (remember, that's everyone from the very involved parent, down to the grumbling tax scold who thinks you spend too much money) base their evaluation of their local school district on a surprisingly small handful of easily identifiable characteristics. Number one on that list—at least, in most of the districts with which we have worked—is perception of teacher quality.

It would be nice if those typical patrons could all agree on what separates a good teacher from one who falls short of the mark. Unfortunately, it's far from that neat and tidy.

In our research, "friends and neighbors" almost always ranks as the top source of school district news. (The definition of "almost always," in this case, is all but two school district patron research projects since 1992.) That means that the folklore about good and not-so-good teachers spreads far and wide across back fences, and over cups of coffee at the local fast food joint. Kind of scary, isn't it?

Insert into this dynamic the idea, expressed by some, that parents and others should be included in formal teacher evaluations, and the school district finds itself in a rather dicey position with several important audiences.

If your school district is faced with this issue, the natural reaction would be to provide exhaustive details about your evaluation process, as a way of saying, "Thanks, but we have it covered." But that misses the point that most patrons with this concern are actually expressing: *we want to know that our input is welcome and valued.*

Recognizing this, the more brand-building response would be to keep parental engagement opportunities front and center in your communications messaging.

A simple repositioning of parent-teacher conferences as more of a relationship-building exercise for parents and teachers sets the stage. Highlighting opportunities throughout the school year when parents can and do offer feedback, and demonstrating how that input has impacted the classroom, the building, and even the district, are also ways to showcase your teamwork philosophy.

If, however, you are pushed into a corner by parents who really do want to participate in teacher evaluations, you'll need to make these "we want to hear from you" messages more formal. Create a protocol (perhaps once a semester) through which interested parents can share their feedback. Report to them that the input has been received and that it "will be provided to the teacher as part of his or her evaluation."

In doing so, you are—again—showing that you value parental input, but in a way that doesn't get you sideways with your teachers (and/or their unions) and with other staff members.

Twenty-First Century Learning Skills

If there's ever a piece of news almost certain to ruffle the feathers of the "back to basics" crowd, it's a school district touting its commitment to instituting so-called Twenty-First Century Learning Skills into the curriculum.

Now, the idea of preparing students with the skills they need to compete in a global economy is pretty hard to argue with, isn't it?

But anyone with an Internet connection and a gripe about what schools are teaching today wouldn't have to do a whole lot of work to discover the touchy-feely side of this academic model and potentially get agitated. Get that ball rolling downhill with the right people in the right school district, and it won't take long for the chatter to start that the schools are "turning their back on the three Rs," or similar ideas.

The best advice, according to our research, is twofold.

First, find ways to attach the expression "Twenty-First Century Learning Skills" to classroom examples, curriculum decisions, and successful outcomes throughout the school district. In other words, make it part of your normal conversation—"getting our students ready to compete means that we need to prepare them with Twenty-First Century Learning Skills, and this new science curriculum does just that"—rather than trying to gin up excitement over some new educational model that is guaranteed to have a segment of your community rolling its eyes and saying, "Here we go again."

Second, over time, begin to inculcate the ideas—like communication, collaboration, and creativity—into your communications. Using the same example from above, "Our students have to learn how to work effectively with each other, and with colleagues near and far, to be able to compete globally in the twenty-first century. This new science curriculum maximizes their opportunities to do just that."

After all, what's the brand goal? Is it to get your patrons saying, "Our school district is committed to Twenty-First Century Learning Skills," or is it to have them see your district's programs evolving to make certain that students have the best chance at success, no matter what label you might attach to such a program? I'm guessing it's the latter.

KEY POINTS

- Hot topics come and go. A school district reaps no brand or patron-relationship rewards from trying to turn its community members into subject matter experts on the latest educational trend.
- As is the case with most any school district news, patrons first want to know what these hot topics mean to them and to their children who attend school in the district (if they have any at the time). Additional details should be available for the smaller percentage of patrons who have a more in-depth level of interest.
- When questions surface about a hot topic, take a step back and work to understand the root of the question first, before answering. Questions about hot topics may sound global in the way they are expressed, but typically surface because of a concern or fear about what the topic might mean to the patron and/or his children.

This is how patrons think: *I need to understand what this latest trend means to me, to my child, to my school, and to the community. Show me, in real-life terms, what is, or will be, different and better as a result of this change. Listen to my concerns, and provide me answers that speak to what matters most to me. Don't sell me. Tell me.*

Chapter Twenty-Three

Special Situations

What Patrons Say They Want and Need in a Crisis

For public relations professionals in any industry, crisis situations stimulate an adrenaline boost like nothing else.

Gathering and sorting information, offering immediate and ongoing counsel, handling media inquiries, keeping and updating a timeline of events, and collecting and shepherding the work of spokespeople all happen at a furious pace.

It's the ultimate acid test of a plan—in this case, a crisis communications plan—in action, and a time when communications professionals often possess never-before-seen influence over decisions that must be made and executed promptly. As a wizened public relations professional once told me about the balance of power during a crisis, "The court of public opinion is meeting today."

When the immediate crisis has subsided, residual communications responsibilities remain, generally for days or weeks, but sometimes for months and even years. What was a frenetic pace becomes more of a situation to be managed. Communications needs and activities evolve as well, matching the pace of new data arrival and target audience interest.

Yet while the urgency typically lessens over time, the basic rule of crisis communications management remains in place, according to patrons who have participated in our school district research: deliver accurate, consistent, audience-focused information at all times (even when the correct answer is, "We don't know, but we're investigating/cooperating/seeking more information" and so on).

For patrons whose school districts are in the midst of an active crisis, their ability to trust the information being disseminated hinges on whether those updates align with their needs—not the district's—combined with whether or not a trusting district-patron relationship exists. For more long-term crises, the quality of the communications response is just as important, they tell us, although the urgency has diminished.

Generally speaking, crises fit into one of three categories:

CRISIS LEVEL 1: IMMEDIATE

An immediate crisis includes any incident (or the discovery of an incident, or a pattern of incidents) that is a "first day" news story in the local media and a subject dominating the discussion in the gabfest at the local coffee shop.

Beyond the obvious incidents that would logically trigger an immediate business and communications response—local law enforcement is involved for whatever reason and/or there are injuries to people and/or there is damage to property, and so on—are events that threaten to create long-term damage to the school district's brand, if not managed effectively.

That's the key element in the definition of an immediate crisis: it's an event.

You have a contentious board meeting that stimulates the first non-unanimous vote on an issue in a decade, and all the back-and-forth from the meeting finds its way into the media.

A teacher publicly challenges your social media rules, and that challenge appears in the media.

A group makes a splash with its solicitation for others to join them in opposing your plan to build a new athletic complex at your high school.

You report the discovery of significant errors in your district's financial records.

Your much-beloved superintendent announces that he or she is ill, and that the prognosis is poor.

You have a booster club that is working behind the scenes to get a coach fired, and their efforts are discovered by your local media.

All these examples can be pinpointed on a calendar or a clock, and a response from the school district will be expected.

It's important to remember that an immediate crisis doesn't have to be a dramatic event involving loss of life, property damage, or anything else that would make it worthwhile for your short-staffed local media to free up a camera crew, still photographer, or reporter: it just has to be something out of the norm that happened, and that needs to be addressed.

Failure to do so, patrons have told us, only heightens their interest and concern. As the expression goes, "Where there's smoke, there's fire." Better to address the smoke, before it can flare up.

What have patrons told us they want in a district's response to an immediate crisis?

Tell me what happened, and why this should matter to me.

This begins with a presentation of the basics from journalism school (who, what, when, where, why, and how) that is focused on the impact on patrons (students, families, staff, and so on) first, and on the district, as a whole, second.

Tell me what you are doing as a result of what happened, and what I need to do, if anything.

Every immediate crisis situation begins with an incident, a pattern of incidents, or the discovery of one or the other, followed by a response. After you report what happened, the next step involves detailing that response in a clear, patron-friendly way. Almost as important: tell patrons what *they* should be doing.

For example, let's say there is a minor bus crash (the incident) on the way to one of your elementary schools one morning. All the students were evaluated on site and cleared by medical personnel to continue on to school on a replacement bus; their school was informed that they would be late; and the staff there got about the business of contacting the parents of the bus riders with the details (the response). Sounds like that's all you need to do, right?

Not exactly. Just reporting the facts to the affected families is only step one. Step two is opening up the lines of communication with that same audience, by inviting questions, and by asking to be kept informed "if your child has questions or concerns."

Doing so makes parents a part of the team that is responding, in a manner of speaking, to this crisis situation and helps you keep your ear to the ground for any post-incident situations that may need attention.

Tell me when you will know more and/or when you will be telling me more.

If the crisis cannot be promptly addressed, then by all means set a time-table for updates. This means describing what information you are working on gathering, when it is expected, and what you will be doing with it once it arrives.

Of course, a lot of this is very crisis-specific. The minor bus crash with no injuries doesn't merit a general update, news conference, or anything else that dramatic; only the parents might need additional information beyond an initial e-mail or phone call.

If you can't decide whether the crisis at hand merits the distribution of further updates, put yourself in the position of the affected audience or audiences. If there are unanswered questions, or opportunities to be suspicious or concerned, it's better to err on the side of overcommunicating, patrons tell us.

Show me your humanity.

Here's where it can get dicey.

The attorneys in the room will want a district to shy away from any statement that could find its way into a court proceeding months or years down the road. For the same reason you don't hop out of the car after a fender bender and say, "That was my fault," school districts have to protect themselves for the future.

However, that doesn't mean that you can't express a measure of humanity in your communications. Patrons have told us in our research that they want to see concern and, where appropriate, compassion when something happens. It helps them feel more connected to their school district when they see it acting more like a human being and less like a business.

Here's all of that advice from patrons, in action:

Rather than:

The members of the board of education are free to vote as they choose, based on what they feel is best for the patrons they represent. It is up to each board member to vote his or her conscience.

How about:

The school district welcomes the active discussion at last night's board of education meeting that led to a 6–1 vote on the matter of placing a bond issue on the ballot in November. These are important decisions that impact our students, their families, our staff, and the community we serve, and we value the fact that ours is an active board that encourages frank discussion of important issues.

Rather than:

We have discovered an error in our financial records from the last two school years. We will provide more information as soon as we complete our investigation.

How about:

Through our ongoing review process, errors in our financial records from the past two school years have been discovered. These errors will not affect our students or their families. While these errors appear to be limited, we are nonetheless continuing to investigate the situation. We will get these issues addressed, and will modify our processes as necessary to prevent this from happening in the future. We will provide an update on our findings within one week, after our investigation concludes.

Rather than:

It has come to our attention that a petition is being circulated seeking to have one of our coaches terminated. All staffing decisions are the responsibility of the school district. Those who sign such a petition should be aware that it will have no impact on those decisions.

How about:

We value the support and enthusiasm of the booster clubs in our school district. We have scheduled a meeting with the leaders of the club that has a concern about coaching, to hear their issues and to review with them the district's processes for selecting and supervising coaches. We look forward to a productive conversation.

And, for more serious issues, rather than:

A school bus traveling to Jefferson Elementary School was involved in a traffic accident this morning. A total of twenty-eight students were on board. Two were taken to the hospital, and the others were transported to school on a replacement bus.

How about:

Two students suffered minor injuries as the result of a traffic accident involving a school bus on the way to Jefferson Elementary School this morning. Those students are currently being evaluated at the hospital.

All parents of students who were on the bus have been notified of the situation, and district personnel are at the hospital with the two students right now. Emergency medical personnel who responded to the accident evaluated all twenty-eight students on board, and recommended transporting two to the hospital for evaluation. We will provide further updates this afternoon, once we have more information.

Notice that in each of the four examples, the factual material presented in the two statements is—with minor wording adjustments for style—mostly the same. The difference is the approach to the rest of the story.

Board discussions are valuable and lead to strong policy. We take the financial errors seriously, but students will not be affected by what has happened. We look forward to talking with the booster club leadership about

their issues. Medical personnel guided the decision-making process regard-
ing the students involved in the bus crash, and we're monitoring the situa-
tion.

Just scratching the surface suggests that more may exist that isn't being
shared. Dig deeper. Put yourself in the position of the audience, and be
guided by what they need to know as you prepare your response.

CRISIS LEVEL 2: ONGOING

It was a toss-up as to whether to call second-level crises "ongoing," or to
flip that coin over and use a more apt description, such as "festering."

**Call them whatever you prefer, these types of crises are either
incidents that hang on after the initial hubbub has long since
passed, or they are situations which well up organically over time.**

Any of the examples from above can linger long enough to eventually be
called an ongoing crisis.

For example, the first non-unanimous vote of the board could lead to a
second, and whispers could begin in your community that there is infighting
that might have serious consequences for students, families, and staff.

Or the financial errors could end up being embezzlement, leading to a
steady stream of questions about processes, who was to blame, and what this
means to students in current and future school years.

Or your mutinous booster club could generate significant support for its
cause, creating an unappetizing mixture of personnel and public relations
issues (particularly if the coach's team runs into a string of bad outings on his
or her particular type of playing surface).

You get the idea: immediate crises necessitate a prompt response. If the
situation remains, or evolves, it may become an ongoing crisis, requiring
further action.

The other type of ongoing crisis rises up organically, meaning that it
seemed like something that could be managed, but morphed into something
altogether different and more challenging.

Attendance-boundary processes fit the description of an organically sur-
facing ongoing crisis.

Many districts use data to explain the thinking behind attendance-boundary changes, and then, believing that all will be well, find themselves
smacked around a bit at a public meeting by people wearing the gear of the
schools that will be impacted. Future public meetings only escalate the issue,
as the same people show up and make the same points over and over again.

We assisted a district with just such a situation, when it came time for
them to move the boundary line that assigned attendance areas to its two high

schools. The facts were clear, the committee had done its work with little fanfare and scant media attention, and the public meeting date was set.

While it would be a stretch to call it a "media situation," there were passionate individuals from both high schools with a bone to pick. We anticipated that situation ahead of time, and eliminated the central microphone set-up in favor of stations in the corners of the room where individuals could share their thoughts. (Those with the biggest beefs visited all four corners, even though there was no benefit to their cause to have their thoughts captured more than once.)

What made it an ongoing crisis was the fact that the attendance-boundary process that had been going along smoothly became more of a story for the local media that evening and, as such, needed to be handled using more of a crisis mindset.

In the case of an ongoing crisis, patrons tell us that they expect their school district to provide the latest information, as it surfaces, in patron-focused language.

The rules don't change; patrons still want to know the pertinent details and what the situation means to them. It's the timing and tone that might need some adjustment.

For instance, in the case of the ongoing board dispute example above, a regular, blow-by-blow update benefits neither the district nor its patrons. When there is news to share, by all means share it, using a tone and style consistent with what's already been presented. Be ready to respond when questions surface, and make certain that everyone on the district's leadership team knows who is doing what when it comes to that response. Otherwise, stand down.

Think, for a moment, about the hot story of the day—either in your community or nationally—that had everyone's interest at the outset, but then dragged on. Notice how the reporting slowed down as well, to better match the pace of actual developments.

Was it lazy journalism that pushed the story off the front page? Hardly. It was the fact that the community of readers, listeners, or viewers had its immediate needs satisfied and became less interested in the minutiae as the story continued. So the reporters kept one eye on the ongoing story while working on the latest issue that was causing the community to chatter.

Ongoing crises have a lot of minutiae. When those details change enough to become news (such as the board making a key decision, not just the board meeting again), be prepared to disseminate details that help move the issue closer to closure, and keep updating your Q&A sheets and other data that appear in the spot reserved for the perpetually curious on your website.

CRISIS LEVEL 3: LEGACY

A crisis achieves legacy status when it becomes part of the folklore of a school district—folklore that rises to the surface whenever something triggers a memory of what took place years or even decades ago.

The quintessential example of a legacy crisis can be found in any rural school district that ever closed an underutilized building. The loss of a school strikes at the very character of a community, calling into question its long-term viability. After all, if there aren't enough families with children to keep the school open, the community's direction is definitely not north.

Fast-forward several years to the same district, now touting its plan to renovate one of its remaining buildings to make it current, and watch the "us versus them" talk resurface.

"Why should we support that plan when they closed *our* school?" and even "If you would *open our school back up*, I might be willing to support your plan."

Other examples of such legacy issues include hard feelings over the change of a high school mascot to something more culturally sensitive, the burr in the saddle caused by the selection of one school's nickname over another following a consolidation, and continued anger over the movement of an attendance-boundary line.

Districts assume that patrons will ultimately recognize the good that has come from the decisions that were made years ago, and get over any perceived snub.

Most of the time, those assumptions would be correct, as life has intervened and other news of the day has buried the feelings of being slighted that were so much on the surface at the time of the event. But, in most communities, all that is required is a trigger to cause those feelings to reappear.

When that trigger happens and the community conversation starts all over again, patrons have told us in our research that the district's best approach is a simple one: relax and respond.

When old wounds become new again—for whatever reason—patrons tell us that school districts that try to "resell" the wisdom of their original decision are missing the point, and are actually causing those with hurt feelings to dig their heels in deeper.

More than anything, in the case of a legacy crisis, patrons say they want validation from their school district.

In other words, they want to feel that their school district understands—and doesn't seek to diminish—their feelings, and doesn't try to defend itself all over again.

Practical individuals know that the school district isn't going to reopen a closed school, won't return the mighty mascot to his or her rightful place (painted on the turf at the 50-yard line, and roaming the sidelines in costume), and won't be shifting the boundaries back to the way they were before. Therefore, there's no reason to replay the process that got the district to where it is today.

So, instead of:

The consolidation of Washington High School into Lincoln High School was a critical cost-saving measure that helped the district maintain its diversity of programming by lowering overhead costs. On the anniversary of the merger, it's important to reflect on all the good that has come as a result of the new Lincoln High School.

Try:

On the anniversary of the merger of two great high schools, we reflect on the traditions that made each of them so special, and on the new traditions being created each and every day by the students and families who now call Lincoln High School home.

Instead of:

While it's clear that the school's previous nickname, the Braves, still has a lot of fans, the district felt that it was disrespectful. The school's current nickname, the Racers, was chosen by a vote of the students at the time, and is now associated with the great teams of Lincoln High School.

Try:

The accomplishments of the student athletes who proudly wore Lincoln High School's former name on their uniforms remain today. While the nickname was changed long ago, the pride in the school displayed by its students, staff, and alumni remains as strong today as it was then.

And instead of:

While there was some expected disagreement about the district's need to move the attendance boundary for the two high schools, ten years later, that decision has proven to be a sound one, as our students in each of the two schools are thriving.

Try:

Ours is a community that has a great sense of tradition, so we understand how difficult it was ten years ago, when an imbalance in the number of students in our two high schools necessitated an adjustment of the attendance boundaries. We continue to work every day to make each high school student's opportunities the best they can possibly be, at both of our high schools.

The differences may seem subtle to school district leaders, but it's powerful to those who are hearing or reading these words. When old wounds surface, it's vital to acknowledge the feelings of those affected and to make a confident (not boastful) statement about life in the district today.

Again, these should be considered talking points to have in the district's "back pocket," if you will, should a patron or your local media bring it up, but not something worthy of proactive attention.

So, what are the events throughout *your* district's history that could be considered legacy crises? If you identify them today, you'll be better prepared when a patron buttonholes you at a basketball game with a comment or question on something you thought they had long since stopped thinking about.

KEY POINTS

- A school district's response to a crisis (both its actual "business" response, and the communications associated with the situation and the response) tells patrons a lot about the trustworthiness of the district and its leadership.
- Communications during a crisis should be focused on what those affected need (and want) to know, blended with details that would be pertinent to a broader audience.
- Immediate crisis situations are events that can be noted on a calendar or a clock. Something has happened, and a response is necessary.
- In an immediate crisis, focus district communication on what happened, how it affects patrons or other audiences, what's being done, and your plans to share more information (if any), along with offering a bit of humanity.
- Ongoing crises are either situations that started as immediate issues and continued on, or crises that surfaced organically as a result of situations that become contentious over time.
- The response to an ongoing crisis should be based on the same checklist of behaviors as for an immediate crisis, tempered by the recognition that not every development may be of interest. True updates that move the story forward merit communication to patrons during an ongoing crisis.
- Legacy crisis situations are typically old wounds from past slights or from unpopular decisions that, for whatever reason, surface again.
- Compassion—not defensiveness—is key in communications associated with a legacy crisis.

This is how patrons think: *Tell me what I need to know, what you are doing about the situation, and when you will tell me more. Show me that you care by what you say and how you say it, focusing more on my information needs than yours.*

Chapter Twenty-Four

Making Your School Communications Program Work

So, there you have it. The collected opinion of patrons since 1992 on what they care passionately about, care somewhat about, and couldn't care less about, generally speaking, when it comes to their school districts.

This research came from districts as small as 438 students, and as large as 25,000 children. From districts whose patrons have the bluest of blood flowing through their veins, to those with free-and-reduced-lunch populations that top 70 percent, and everything in between. From districts that are growing, those that are maintaining, and those that are barely hanging on.

Each piece of data shared in this book was collected for the purpose of helping an individual school district understand where its patrons think it excels, where they think it's performing acceptably (if not at an exemplary level), and where they think it falls short of the mark.

In analyzing this data since we began our work, it became clear that certain subjects routinely drew a lot of attention, while others did not. Certain areas also generated a lot of specific comments, which suggested quite clearly just how strong the interest was in these topics, while some others barely registered a pulse.

That analysis produced the three tiers that you see on the Patron Information Pyramid, dividing the possible subjects a school district *could* advance to its patrons into categories based on the average interest level of patrons across all types of school districts.

In any such analysis, there is a margin of error. In other words, as was mentioned earlier, you may have seen some areas that you thought needed to move up into a higher tier and others that maybe should be moved down, based on what you know about your district.

That's good. Your district is unique, and it may have specific circumstances that put it outside of the overall average—either all the time or episodically.

Where I would suggest you hold fast to the guidance you see in the Pyramid is at the top level. While there are some modest variations from district to district on the topics in the middle and bottom levels, there was an unerring consistency at the highest level—no matter what the district's geography or demography.

In other words, you can't go wrong focusing your communications on teachers, on how you spend tax dollars, on preparing students for their futures, and so on. This is how patrons judge the quality of their local school district first, so giving them as many pieces of evidence as possible about those topics is always a good strategy.

That doesn't mean that you can't add to the list to make it a better match for your district's patrons. It's just that the top tier, as specified, is a good place to start.

That's the key to making these research findings work for your school district as you seek to build and nurture a stronger relationship with your patrons: *use them as a guide, not as a precise recipe.*

You should also recognize that whatever Pyramid structure you believe fits your school district today, it will evolve.

Be sure to keep your eyes and ears open to all the channels that provide you data, so you can track that evolution. Don't rely exclusively on the people you hear from all the time. Ask your teachers to be listening and to share what they are hearing. If you discover an issue, address it. If it becomes a trend, you may need to revise your communications strategy.

Above all, put every piece of news and information you want to share through a tough test: would a typical patron care, *or do I just want them to care?*

If you want them to care, you're not communicating. If they care (or if you can adjust how you present the information so it fits what they do care about), then you *are* communicating.

So what can you do to make the most of this information in your district?

STEP 1: CONDUCT A COMMUNICATIONS AUDIT— START BY REVIEWING YOUR OUTBOUND COMMUNICATIONS

We've had the pleasure of working with numerous districts on communications audits, and they can be particularly eye-opening.

Simply put, a communications audit *starts* with a comprehensive analysis of all print and electronic materials disseminated by a school district over a set time period—generally eighteen to twenty-four months—to determine the themes, topics, and even turns of phrase that seem to appear over and over again. Identifying these (and evaluating the consistency with which style issues, such as logos, are utilized) helps to pinpoint the "face" that a school district is presenting.

For example, does your district tend to focus on communicating about excellence? Student achievement? Fiscal efficiency? Something else?

It's likely that you'll see several themes repeated frequently—generally woven into the fabric of what you disseminate, rather than screaming in obvious language off the printed page. Take the time you need to determine what these themes are, and see how they match up to what you *think* you are saying (or what you'd like to be saying).

That's the eye-opening part of this analysis. You may be telling good stories, but are they helping to build the brand you want?

STEP 2: CONDUCT A COMMUNICATIONS AUDIT—THEN ASK YOUR PATRONS

Once you have identified the themes found regularly in what you are putting into the patron arena, it's time to find out what those same patrons are actually seeing, hearing, reading, and—most importantly—feeling about the school district.

It's a bit like the old "telephone" game from your youth. One person whispers something into the ear of the person sitting next to him or her, and that person sends the message to the next person, and the process continues around a circle of friends. Unless the individuals are disciplined, the chances are good that the message will undergo some radical change between the original sender and the final receiver.

That's the way it is with patrons. Their attention spans are short, and their focus is fuzzy. What you think you are saying, they may not be hearing the same way.

The only way to know for certain is to ask. Doing so helps you pinpoint the gap between the brand you *believe* you have and the one you really have.

You can do so in one of two ways: qualitative (such as focus groups) and quantitative (a survey).

We recently had the chance to conduct focus groups for a school district that wanted to evaluate how its patrons perceived its brand. The challenge was that it was an older community, with less than 20 percent of the households having current students. They'd been supportive of the district in the past, but how do they feel about the district today, now that they no longer have any students bringing home report cards? What is their brand perception?

What we discovered was a community that continued to appreciate how the district "handled its business." The evidence cited was the steady-as-she-goes leadership of the administrative team, the absence of bad news stories in the paper, good reports about the classroom performance of students, and the fact that the school buildings looked like someone cared. That was how they remembered their own students' school experiences (for those who had children who had attended school in the same district in the past), and they appreciated the fact that the district continued to have that commitment.

Boil that down, and the idea was simple: the patrons appreciated the district's sense of *tradition*.

This insight provided the clue that the school district needed to begin reshaping their communication program to take those "top of the Pyramid" topics—and a few others specific to the district—and recast them to fit the brand image that patrons already had.

This process involved a detailed series of focus groups with different stakeholder groups, to hear these select individuals share their stories and their thoughts.

If, however, you'd rather have a statistical review of patron opinion, then a quantitative type of approach, such as a telephone or online survey, is the way to go.

In such a survey, you have patrons evaluate the people, programs, facilities, and district-patron relationship factors of your district, to get a sense of where they believe you shine, where your performance is acceptable, if not stellar, and where they think you're less than exemplary. All of that is key brand data, because it says whether they think you are the district "with great teachers that turns out great kids," the one that "doesn't offer good value for my tax money," or something else.

You might also pair the evaluation questions with a section asking patrons to state their level of agreement with a series of statements about what "most patrons think." For example, do they agree or disagree that most patrons think that the teachers are among the best in the region? Or that the district makes good use of tax dollars? Or that recent building projects were necessary?

By asking patrons to state what they believe "most patrons think," you're actually asking them to state what *they* think—without putting them on the spot. It's a great technique that really helps to dissect the thought process of patrons, and we've seen it work wonders for districts.

Either way (qualitative or quantitative) will give you insight into how your specific patrons think and how their thinking matches with yours. It's mostly a matter of whether you'd like to hear the voice of your patrons live and in person, or you'd rather ask them to put their hands up and be counted via a survey (and some districts employ both methodologies).

STEP 3: CREATE A COMMUNICATIONS PLAN

Once you can pinpoint the gaps between how you are expressing your brand and how it is being received, it's time to put together a communications plan.

If the thought of yet another plan sends shivers down your spine, don't worry. You don't have to create something that's surely destined to gather dust after it is bound and stuck on a high shelf.

Just start by identifying the key ideas you want to express during the coming year (or school year—your choice). Then, identify ways in which you might get those messages out, and how you will judge whether or not they have been received in the way you hope they are.

For example, if you want to make certain that your patrons have a deeper understanding of your facility needs and challenges—because you're going to be asking for their support for a bond issue for new buildings in about two years—you might identify a communications objective to "begin telling the facility-need story."

You could then pinpoint some key components of that story (building challenges, cost to renovate versus build new, etc.) that you could disseminate at various points during the year—either as stand-alone stories, or as subordinate messages in other stories.

Whatever the case, just enumerating the key things that you want patrons to know by the time the year is up will help to discipline your work and to focus your resources where they will be most effective.

In this example, it's a story that matches two items from the top level of the Pyramid: use of tax dollars, and maintenance and upkeep of buildings. But what if you have what you think is a key communications objective that also happens to fall well below the top level?

Not to worry. As I mentioned earlier, the Pyramid is a *guide* that you need to personalize to make it fit your district's unique characteristics; it is not a set of handcuffs. The items in the top tier should be priorities, but you will likely have one or more topics from the other tiers that make an appearance in your plan.

The best strategy is to list all your objectives and then compare them to the Pyramid. The red flag would be if you found that in your list of objectives, the items that fit in the second and third tiers outnumber those that fit in the top group.

Again, it's not a hard-and-fast rule. But if your list doesn't pass the "eyeball test," then you're probably pushing out too much information *you* care about, at the expense of information that your patrons care about.

This is just a rudimentary approach to communications planning. But it's a good start. If you get totally enthused and need to see something more formal, there are more complex approaches as well. The key is just to get started.

STEP 4: CHECK YOUR PROGRESS AND UPDATE YOUR PLAN

There's no need to be manic about it (in terms of the calendar), but you should plan to regularly check on whether or not your communications are syncing with what matters to your patrons.

One easy way to do this is to run occasional online surveys. There are services (Survey Monkey and Zoomerang, to name a couple) out there that offer you great tools, which are easy to use and very inexpensive. (But I wouldn't recommend that you limit yourself to only the free versions of any service. They have extreme limitations on what you can do, and therefore really don't offer much in the way of utility for a school district. Plus, the annual fees for the more feature-rich versions tend to be extremely reasonable.)

If you take this route, remember that online surveys are not the same as telephone surveys. By that I mean that the data in online surveys come only from people who choose to participate, and many of these individuals are the same people who always show up for board meetings, always volunteer, always send you e-mails, and so on. It's not a true cross-section, but it does let you keep your finger on the pulse of your most interested patrons. And it's great PR to always be asking patrons how the district is performing.

If you want something more robust, a telephone survey is the way to go. But again, don't expect to see big changes in the short term. As I've said throughout this book, your typical patron doesn't pay close attention, so don't expect to see much needle movement in the first year or so.

STEP 5: STEADY AS SHE GOES

While you may have some course corrections along the way (particularly for more temporary communications issues), you should keep in mind the old saying about it being "a marathon, not a sprint."

If your objective is to provide truly brand-building communications, then you'll need patience and a steady hand to keep sending out information on the same subject matter month after month—because it's what interests your patrons—no matter how fatigued you may get with the messages. It will test your patience, but remember that just when you think you can't take it any longer, your patrons are finally starting to absorb bits and pieces of what you are trying to say.

Chapter Twenty-Five

Some Final Thoughts

I've been fortunate enough to work with people from large and small companies, not-for-profits and major international for-profit enterprises, municipalities, fire districts, and school people. And I can tell you, without hesitation, that there's nobody who loves what they do more than school people do.

Since 1992, I've seen that professional dedication at work in meeting rooms with paneling and carpet that had been there since the 1960s, and in grand theaters that doubled as school board meeting rooms, complete with every piece of electronics you could want for displaying my little old Power-Point presentation.

The one constant, no matter where the district is located, is that school people understand how important their profession is to every child, every family, and every community. They live, eat, sleep, and breathe public education. It is an absolute joy for me to be in the presence of such passionate professionals.

In writing this book, my goal was to help you maximize the resources you apply toward building and nurturing the strong patron relationships that are critical to your school district, by more effectively focusing your communications efforts.

While I know from working with you that there is so much you *could* tell patrons about the great things that are happening in your school district, you know from experience that they don't listen to everything you say.

That leaves two choices: keep telling them what you think is important, or concentrate your efforts on subjects that matter to them.

Because of your enthusiasm for your work, it's natural to assume that your patrons will eventually pay attention to anything you say, if you just keep talking. But it doesn't play out that way (and we have the data to prove it), and you risk having your patrons eventually tune you out, if you keep talking about topics that just aren't on their radar.

You'll do yourself and your district a big favor by focusing your efforts primarily on the issues that always seem to generate interest across all districts, and supplement that core list with topics that are unique to your district—and that are of interest to your patrons.

Do so, and your communications will work harder, smarter, and better than ever before.